CW01083570

MEMORIES OF

Atherstone

MEMORIES OF

Atherstone

Christine Freeman

TEMPUS

Born in February 1912 in Atherstone, Sidney R.S. Barnes is an ardent writer and keen photographer of subjects relating to the locality for a period of around sixty years. He has written many papers and books on local historical buildings, events and projects, and one could safely say that collecting old photographs and information relating to the local area is one of Sid's main interests, one which has seen him become a well-known authority on such matters. Over the years Sid has always been prepared to share or loan photographs from his wonderful personal archives to many individuals, groups and organisations. It is with the utmost respect and admiration for his work that I dedicate my book to him.

First published 2005

Tempus Publishing Limited
The Mill, Brimscombe Port,
Stroud, Gloucestershire, GL5 2QG
© Christine Freeman, 2005

British Library Cataloguing in Publication Data.
A catalogue record for this book is available from the British Library.

ISBN 0 7524 3422 5

Typesetting and origination by Tempus Publishing Limited
Printed in Great Britain

Contents

Acknowledgements

I would like to thank most sincerely the following people for sharing their memories, life experiences and photographs. Their recollections have evolved into a unique publication, capturing the essence of Atherstone's past for future generations:

Gary Albrighton, Gladys Allcock, Roy Allitt, Sidney Barnes, Maureen Barnes, Gerry Barnes, Jean Beale, Rita Bernard, George Blower, Derek Booton, Bracebridge Court, Janice Breedan Mona Budge, Sylvia Rose Burgess, Geoff Butler, Edward Byard, Amirian Byard, Trevor and Margaret Chapman, Dorothy Cheshire, Eileen Colclough, Charles and Beryl Cooke, Bill Cooper, Rita Deeming, Valda Deeming, Wilf Deeming, Emily Dewis, Janet Dingley, Bill Dixon, Horace Doherty, Maurice Douglas, Gerald Eaton, Milly Evans, Denis Fletcher, Bill Ford, Val Ford, Joe Ford, Mimmie Fowkes, Cynthia Fox, Beryl Freeman, John Freeman, Malc Freeman, Pat Fryer, Ralph Fryer, Beryl Gilliver, Ernest Good, Gordon Gudger, Ella Harrison, Ted Hatwell, Iris Healey, Gwen Heath, Ernest Hobby, Doris Holland, Tom Issitt, Gladys Jewell, Eveline Johnson, Gwen Johnson, Margaret Killian, George Knight, Nancy, Ron and Sylvia Lees, Beattie McCarthy, Ellen Mills, Jean Mills, Tricia Milne, Stuart Morcom, George Morris, Phyllis Morris, Margaret Neale, Claire Neville, Jean Neville, Irene Northall, Margaret Owen, Steve Owen, Sue Owen, Joyce Peart, Valerie Pickard, Sidney Pratt, Joyce Reading, Keith Reynolds, Charlie Ross, Bill Rowntree, Dorothy Rushton, Bet Russell, David Russell, Celestine and Derek Smith, Marilyn Smith, Paul Smith, John Spragg, Elsie Swann, Milly Thumbwood, Mavis Turner, Clifford Vero, Ray Walker, Dorothy Walton, Hilda Whelan, Jane Wykes, Margaret Wykes.

I would also like to thank Dr Alan Barnes for his continued support and advice; Tania Marshall (my daughter) for the endless hours she has spent typing up my original handwritten manuscripts; Avril Breedon and all of the Atherstone Library staff for their inspirational support.

Finally I would like to thank Matilda Pearce and everyone at Tempus Publishing for their guidance with the compilation of this publication.

Introduction

Nearly 2,000 years have passed since the Romans built the famous Watling Street from London to Chester – by way of St Albans and Lichfield.

The mile-long stretch of the Watling Street through Atherstone is known today as Long Street. Houses and businesses of various trades developed here over time to create a vibrant community at the heart of Atherstone. In 1850 there were thirty-two alehouses named in a *Historical Gazetteer* belonging to the late Mr W. Orton of Atherstone. In addition to these there were nine brew houses which brewed their own beer. Although little has changed in the streets' outward appearance, there has been mass demolition of buildings in the town since the 1940s, including the yards, of which there were once over fifty, and small courts. The town was surrounded by open fields but with very little land available for building on. Land was eventually purchased by Atherstone Council on which to build new housing estates in the 1930s, a time when Britain's slums were being cleared. The families who lived in the yards and other areas of the town were gradually rehoused.

The yards and small courts in Long Street continued to develop with time. Each yard was named after the alehouse, trade or business that was adjacent to the front of the yard in Long Street and Market Street.

With the invention of steam power many of the hat factories, for which Atherstone is renowned, were built. Atherstone was the ideal location due to the streams and position of the canal to transport coal and goods. This in turn led to an increase in the local population, and the demand for housing resulted in the hurried building of new homes, which were mostly inadequate. People do however recall some very happy times spent living in the yards. They grew up together, played together and worked together. And, as one lady recalls, they cried together too.

Coal mining was a main local industry in the area, with Baddesley Colliery situated just over two miles from Atherstone. Both the hatting industry and coal mining had diminished by the 1990s. There are two hat factories standing today, both empty and dilapidated – Hatton's factory, situated behind Gale's newsagents in Long Street, and Wilson & Staffords in Coleshill Road. Atherstone housed other fashion factories in the town by the 1950s – slippers, braces, stockings, knitwear, shoes and boots and lingerie were all manufactured here. These industries had disappeared by the late 1980s. So too did the unique social life, where workers would organise their own sporting contests, day trips and parties.

Sale & Son, the seed and corn merchants, traded in South Street and Owen Street until 1968. The Cattle Market was situated in Station Street where the car park now stands opposite the rear of the Co-op store in Long Street. Atherstone town centre was very much a place where its inhabitants lived side by side with industry and agriculture.

Many of Atherstone's important buildings have disappeared over the years. The Town Hall stood in the Market Square for over 200 years before it was demolished in 1963. Atherstone Hall had stood in beautiful grounds behind St Mary's church until it was demolished in 1964. Both buildings had accommodated the townsfolk in many different ways. The Picturedrome in Long Street was demolished in the 1960s, and in the late 1980s the more modern cinema – The Regal, which opened its doors in the 1950s – was also demolished. The Miners Welfare was demolished after the closure of Baddesley Colliery in 1989. The Atherstone train station has been used as offices since its closure over twenty years ago.

The new A5 road was constructed on open fields, which bypassed Atherstone town centre in the 1960s. Distribution warehouses and other trade units have developed here, on the two Industrial Estates either end of the bypass, namely Carlyon Road and Holly Lane.

The sounds of the factory hooters, the clip-clopping of the horse's hooves, the tapping of the blacksmith's anvil and the chattering of the factory workers going to and from work have all disappeared into an ever-changing world. However, amidst all the changes that have taken place, Atherstone remains a close-knit community and the town still stands in the heart of charming rural countryside, which is mostly unchanged.

one
The War Years

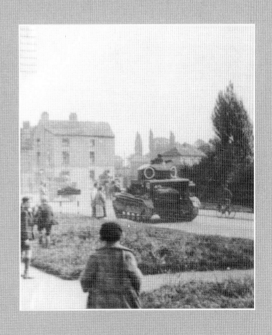

The First World War 1914-1918

Dad bought Old Bob back

Whilst living at Cottage Farm, Birchley Heath, war with Germany broke out and lasted about four years. At the beginning there was a shortage of food. People were getting desperate. Then the government took control. Dad was told to churn his milk and make butter, but the government would commandeer the butter. The milk was put through a separator, the skimmed milk gushed out while the cream dripped through. Dad was ordered to feed the skimmed milk to the piglets to produce pork for the butchers.

This war was not mechanised – tanks etc. had not been invented until the war was nearly at an end. What large guns our Army did have had to be pulled by horses, and this left a shortage of horses on the farms. Old Bob was sent to the war, but when the tanks and mobile trucks were mechanised, the horses that were left were sent home. I remember there was a large sale of horses. Dad went and bought back Old Bob, whom we loved. The sale was held in the Atherstone Cattle Market, which is now a car park. The children were amused whenever there was a thunderstorm, as Old Bob would gallop along and kick out his legs. He thought he was back at the war,

horses are very sensitive. My dad would talk to him and try to calm him down when he was frightened by noises.

It was a case of man fighting man in the trenches. The men were slaughtered – terrible loss of life and practically every family lost someone. There were few men left behind so that old men, children and mainly women had to do the work on the home front, and they had to work very long hours. Dad did not go, as he had to work on all the surrounding farms and do other work, which left mother with terrific burdens, such as carrying heavy buckets of food to the piglets. My mother was seven months pregnant at the time, the workload resulted with my sister being born two months prematurely.

Mimmie Fowkes

They told my granny my dad had been killed

The War Office in London wrote and told my granny that my dad had been killed, they sent her a £6 1s money order with the letter. My dad's name appeared in *The Birmingham Post* newspaper, which my granny kept, but it's a bit tatty now. Later, my dad was listed as a prisoner of war in Germany and my granny wrote to the War Office about it. They apologised for the error and asked for the money back.

Maureen Barnes

Euphoria of fireworks

I was serving with the Gloucestershire Regiment when my Commanding Officer told me to go into a village in France to fetch supplies. He ordered me to stay on the road and not to go off it, or I would get lost. I continued on the road with my horse and wagon when all of a sudden shells were fired above my head. I turned off the road out of the way amongst the trees. To my horror the bodies of hundreds of men were lying dead on the ground. I managed to get back onto the road. My mind went blank and the next thing I remember was being carried on a stretcher by two comrades. In the night sky above me was a euphoria of 'fireworks'. What a wonderful sight it was, I stared in amazement. It wasn't until I recovered that I realised I'd been shell-shocked. The fireworks had actually been live ammunition, exploding and lighting up the sky above my head. I was one of the lucky ones to survive the First World War.

Ernest Hobby

Private Henry Jones, who served in the First World War.

George Lees, who served with the King's Own Rifle Regiment.

The khaki-clad figure

I was born in the small industrial town of Atherstone in 1910 in Southwood House, situated at the corner of South Street and Welcome Street. I was the youngest member of the family and the only girl. I had four older brothers – Joe, Gerald, Harold and Kingsley. The eldest, Joe, was apprenticed to a tailor in Leicester and once, when he returned home at the weekend, I remember telling my father that I was not going to sit next to him as he was 'stale' and my brother was 'fresh'. Father abominated fresh bread as it gave him indigestion and he always ate stale bread, so I was familiar with those adjectives. I was about four at the time. Soon after this we moved to a three-storey Georgian house called Irvine House, in Long Street. It had a stone staircase with wide shallow steps, a stone paved hall and a front door possessing a large iron knocker. During the First World War I remember hearing the banging of this knocker in the middle of the night. On hearing my mother running down stairs to open the door I peeped over the banister to see the khaki-clad figure of my brother, home on leave from France.

Sylvia Rose Burgess

Left: Charles Lees, George Lees' brother, served with the Warwickshire Regiment. The photograph is surrounded with Past Battle Honours. Charles and his brother William were both 'killed in action'.

Lillie Bucknell, George Lees' wife, is seen here centre front with munitions workers during the First World War.

The nurse taught Joe how to do cross stitch

Dressing up with a younger friend and playing at 'dolls' was always popular. I only wanted the one doll I had, which had belonged to an older cousin, Muriel Denham. It was of German origin and had a pink and white face and fair hair. My brother Joe gave me a little coat for it that he had made at the tailor's where he worked, in Leicester. He had to guess the measurements, which he did correctly. When he was recovering from typhoid fever, in a hospital in France during the war, he also embroidered a pram cover for it, with cross-stitch, of which I was very proud as it bore my initials – R. A. (Rosie Austin). The nurse had taught him how to do cross-stitch. My mother went out to visit him and he gave it to her for me.

Sylvia Rose Burgess

They came over in a coal boat

My mother, Anna Marie, came over to England with her family and lots of other Belgians when the First World War started. They were as black as the ace of spades when they got to England – they came across the sea in a coal boat. I don't know how the family came to live in Atherstone, as it was a good way from the coast. Some of the family went back to Belgium when the war ended. My mother married my dad and stayed here.

Celestine Bonner

Postcards sent in the First World War

To, Annie –

County of London War Hospital, Epsom,
'I landed here yesterday from France and I am
feeling pretty well'. Fred xxxx

With Best Wishes – From Daddy
x x x x x
Somewhere in France on Active Service
March 3rd – 1918

Folkestone, 19 February 1918

Dear Lizzie,
I am going across this afternoon and thought
you would like a line or two. It is lovely here
and close to the sea, hope you will go and visit
A. and H. It is a great comfort to me to know
they have good friends. I am going on alright.
There are hundreds of different reg soldiers
going across.
From Ernie

The photograph of the Hospital Ship that Fred sent to Annie.

The Atherstone Church Lads' Brigade marching up Coleshill Road to commemorate the end of the First World War, November 1918.

Atherstone Peace Celebrations in 1919, showing The Clock Inn and the Ram yard entrance.

The Second World War 1939-1945

Marching through the wicket gate

Trains would be heard at the train station in the early hours of the morning. Prisoners of war would be marched through the wicket gate at the rear of the train station. The sound of their steel-studded boots could be heard along the Old Watling Street, under the cattle arch up to and past the Kings Head towards the gates of Merevale Park prisoner-of-war camp.

Gary Albrighton

The streets were paved with gold

I had embarked on a new career as a fireman, but during the Second World War I was called back into my old regiment – The Seaforth Highlanders. We had to collect the prisoners of war from Arbury and Merevale Park POW camps and supervise them throughout the working day. When Coventry was blitzed, we worked for three days amongst the rubble. We had to recover jewellery that had been disseminated into the streets from the shops in the city centre. The streets were literally paved with gold. The most humiliating experience I ever had was when we were all strip-searched at the end of each day along with the POWs in case any jewellery had been stolen.

Tom Issitt

Come down the mountain

I was born in Arlesey, Bedfordshire, and enlisted into the Hertfordshire and Bedfordshire Regiment the day that war was declared, along with six of my friends. I was Tank Commander No. 5952619 and in charge of seven tanks of the Bren Gun Tank Carrier Platoon. The battalion consisted of 1,000 soldiers and the division totalled some 60,000 soldiers, known as the Herts and Beds. The lads from London were called the Eastenders. When we came to Atherstone we were stationed at Merevale Park POW camp. I met and married a local girl named Irene Clark. I'd often drive a tank from the camp up to Irene's house in Stratford Avenue to see her. One night I overturned the tank around the tiny island in the middle of the road, right by the house where Irene lived. I was injured, I hurt my back and was admitted into Birmingham hospital. The Captain gave permission for another soldier

Ernest Lawrence Good, who served in the Second World War.

Ernest Good, Wally Summer and Ernie Warren. This photograph was taken at Merevale Park POW camp.

The Bren Gun Tank Carrier Platoon convoying towards the Blue Boar Inn, Witherley Road.

from my platoon to bring Irene to the hospital to see me in the Captain's car. On another occasion I was late getting back to the camp and Irene's dad said, 'here wear this big overcoat and trilby and pull the collar right up to disguise yourself.' I actually got away with it, they let me through the gates without any questions. They must have thought I was someone very important!

Irene and I were married at Atherstone when I was given leave. One night a bomb had been dropped near to the camp and we were ordered to move quickly northwards. We never knew where we would be called to go. Our army manoeuvres took place in Asia, Singapore, Malaya, Bangkok and Burma. Our platoon was high on a mountain when a Frenchman came to tell us that the war

had been over for days! He told us to 'come down the mountain to the POW camp, at least you will get fed.' The Frenchman made arrangements for the train to come up the mountain and fetch us down. When we finally returned home to England I weighed about six stone.

Ernest Lawrence Good

Stalag XB

I joined up with the North Staffordshire Regiment in 1939. While we were in Normandy trying to capture Caen the whole company lost their lives, how I survived I'll never understand. I was transferred to the Worcestershire Regiment as a Quartermaster Sergeant. We got 'cut up' again with the

Left: Charles Cooke (right) with an Army pal.

Opposite above: The Nijmegan power station, Holland.

Opposite below: The bridge at Arnhem, Holland. It was the one bridge that was not captured by British or American forces; the Allied attempt to take the bridge was dramatised in the film *A Bridge Too Far*.

Charles Cooke driving his jeep in Germany.

2nd Army when we were with General Horrocks in Nijmegan. I had a big surprise when I was at Nijmegan power station. There were British and American soldiers there and out of all those men, I came face to face with Les Billingham, an Atherstone lad. He was a dispatch rider at the power station.

As we made our way across Northern Germany we arrived at a concentration camp, Stalag XB, approximately fifteen miles north of Belsen. British and American soldiers had been captured in the German retreat. The camp was supposed to contain political prisoners. There were piles of bodies, thousands of men had been flung in and left to die. The prisoners were pitiful, weak, starving and diseased, and were clinging to life when we got there. German men and women were collected in lorries to clean up the camp. The women scrubbed the filthy huts and cleaned up the survivors, before being sent to the hospital. Those who were dead were laid out for burial. The men dug mass graves for the dead. When the Stalag XB camp was finally cleared, it was burned to the ground.

Charles Cooke

The German's confiscated film

I decided I would join the Royal Navy when the war broke out. I was on the HMS *Griffin*, they were a great crew. When times went a bit quiet we amused ourselves, we had a competition to see who could grow the longest beard. Our captain stopped the ship once to let some pigeons settle. The pigeons ate chocolate out of our hands. We didn't want to kill them to eat, as we enjoyed having them aboard. We confiscated a captured German soldier's film out of his camera and got the film developed. When the HMS *Codrington*, a C-class Destroyer, was sunk, we managed

German paratroopers landing in Crete, May 1941.

An Italian Destroyer with a German crew.

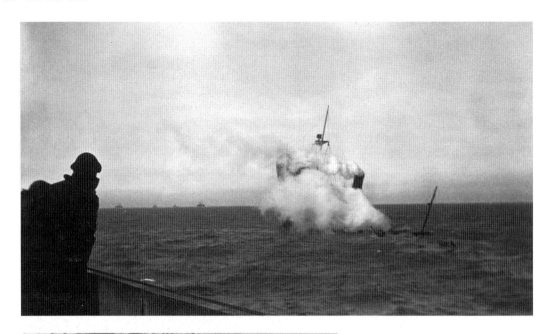

Above: One of our ships, possibly HMS *Codrington*, going down.

Left: HMS *Griffin* with survivors from HMS *Codrington*, a C-class Destroyer.

The crew of HMS *Griffin* taking a few days' respite, 1941.

A German U-boat which surrendered to HMS *Lowerstoft* on 5 June 1945.

Wilf Deeming.

to rescue some of its crew. George Gregory, an Atherstone lad, was on the ship when it sunk. We tried so hard to find him but were unsuccessful.

Wilf Deeming

Juno Beach

I served in the Royal Navy during the Second World War on the HMS *Devonshire*. For nine weeks the HMS *Devonshire* was one of a fleet of ships who mortared the Germans, who were bunkered in their huts along the beaches of France. There were British and Canadian soldiers attached to the HMS *Devonshire*. In June 1944 the tank landing crafts packed full of soldiers began to cross over to the French beaches. Juno Beach was the destination for the soldiers attached to our ship.

Edward Arthur (Mick) Byard

LACW Constance Adcock

Leading Aircraftwoman (LACW) Constance Adcock, No. 2063210, joined the Women's Royal Air Force Nursing Corps in February 1942 and served until April 1946. Constance had an older brother, Ralph, who was with the Warwickshire Regiment out in Burma during the war. LACW Constance Adcock received the Pacific Star (Burma) and the Defence Medal (King's commendation for brave conduct). She kept her medals in the original boxes that they were posted to her in.

Margaret Neale

Stationed at Mons Barracks, Aldershot

When I was working at Denham's hat factory during the war, I joined the ATS for two and a half years. I was stationed at Aldershot as a cook – 'Cook in Charge'. I was at Mons Barracks, the Officer Cadet Training Unit.

Above left: LACW Constance Adcock.

Above right: Edward Arthur (Mick) Byard.

Right: The Canadian Winnipeg Rifle Regiment aboard one of the landing crafts of the HMS *Devonshire* prior to crossing towards Juno Beach on D-Day 1944.

There were 600 soldiers at the barracks – male and female. We all did the church parade every Sunday morning, I loved going on parade. Not everyone went, obviously, there were soldiers who had to do Guard Duty at the barracks while we were on parade. When I was demobbed, I got married and returned to work at Denham's.

Beryl Gilliver

Uncle Wal and my dad at Dunkirk

My dad and my uncle Walter joined the Coldstream Guards in 1928 and 1929 – in peacetime. In 1940 they were called up on the Army Reserve list, due to them being trained soldiers. I remember both their Army numbers – my dad was No. 2653541 and uncle Wal was No. 2654604, how's that! They were called up as soon as the war started. My dad was twenty-nine years old and my uncle Wal was thirty-one years old. My dad went into the 1st Battalion and uncle Wal went into the headquarters of the Guards' Armoured Brigade. Hundreds of soldiers were scrambling onto boats and crafts trying to get to safety at Dunkirk. My dad and my uncle Wal were amongst some of the last to leave. In the end my dad said 'come on, we ain't going to get captured. We are going to get killed if we stay here any longer'. Although my dad was the youngest, uncle Wal always did what my dad said. They chucked their rifles, boots, belts and everything else down and swam out till they got on a boat. They ended up in Scarborough.

Derek Smith

Cheese for woodbines

Rationing went on for years, during and after the war. The miners got double the amount of cheese. Instead of 2oz they got 4oz because they needed it for their sandwiches. One of them who had got no money asked my dad, 'Can I have five woodbines? I've got no money but I can give you my cheese'. You got points for tinned stuff and units for bread. I was always asking my dad if I could have his clothing and sweet coupons. At The Woodman we had stables at the back, when the cattle sale was on they would stable the horses there. During the war my dad reared pigs in our yard and the inspector would come and see how much we had. We were only allowed to keep so much for ourselves, we did help other people out too. We used to have sides of bacon, hams and chicklings. Someone from the slaughterhouse used to come and slaughter the pigs. The blood used to be caught in a bowl to make faggots and black pudding. We took loads of evacuees in due to all the rooms we had at the pub. I remember we took in four Phillipinos who were drilling for coal, they were Diamond Drillers. When the air raids were on we all used to sleep in the cellar.

Jean Beale

A city kid in a market town

Evacuees were brought to the train station where a lady would meet them all and walk around the town to see who could take them in. My mother took in Derek Knowles, he was about five years old. He was a lovely lad from Coventry. At the back of our house, up the entry, my granny kept chickens in a shed that she used to call 'the old place'. One day Derek couldn't be found anywhere, granny searched high and low. When my granny eventually found him he was watching the chickens in 'the old place'. When she asked him what he was doing there, he said 'I'm waiting to see how the chicken stamps the lion onto the egg.' My granny couldn't stop laughing, it must have been so different for him living in Atherstone compared to Coventry.

Val Ford

Air Raid Precautions, Sheepy Road. From left to right are Olive Archer, -?-, Jean Beale, Isabelle Lawton, Hetty Rowntree. -?-.

The ARPs

We used to go to learn our fire practice in Sheepy Road, near the cemetery. One of us would have a bucket, one would pump the water through, while the other one would have to lie down and put the fire out with the hose. We did this practice in case incendiary bombs were dropped.

Jean Beale

When the snow was knee deep

I can remember the displaced persons shovelling the snow in Long Street. They had to take it down to Kings Avenue by horse and cart. There was a great big mountain of snow in the finish. It was there for months, it didn't thaw out for a long time. We made slides, there was loads of kids, it was great fun.

Ray Walker

The blackout

We had black blinds at the windows inside the house and shutters on the outside. People had to make the shutters themselves out of pieces of wood. When the Germans dropped their bombs in Baddesley the pit baths were damaged. A bomb landed in Baddesley Wood. Maypole Lane and Carts Lane got hit, and houses had their windows blown out and roofs blown off. Two people were killed, one was an evacuee.

Maurice Douglas

The luminous pink pig

It was one of the nights after the war was declared over. It was either VE Day or VJ Day – Victory in Europe and Victory in Japan. I can remember it being a very warm night. I was sitting on my uncle's shoulders and remember seeing the tops of people's heads. We were up the Market Street outside Bates' butchers. I was born in the first year of the war so I would have been five years old at the time. All of a sudden I saw this bright pink pig lit up. The outline of the pigs face was a luminous electric pink light. I had never seen anything like it in my life. Thinking about it, I had not seen a street lamp lit up or car headlights – I only ever knew the nights to be pitch black.

I used to go to Vero's Dairy in Long Street with my mum and Auntie. Pictures of fancy biscuits and cakes were painted onto metal square sheets, dotted around the shop. 'We used to have those before the war', they would say to me. I used to look at them both sideways, because I didn't believe them. They didn't look real enough, I'd only ever seen plain biscuits and cakes.

Valerie Pickard

A good old sing-song

I can remember when we first came to Atherstone – I couldn't get over how many pubs there were. Every few yards there was

The Square and Compass (now The Blue Dog), in Station Street.

a pub! I had never seen so many in any one place. My favourite was the Square and Compass, we used to have a right good old sing-song. Someone played the piano in there every Saturday night.

Ernest Lawrence Good

In the mood

Stan Green, who used to have the paper shop, now Gales in Long Street, had a four- piece band. They played at the Town Hall and the Co-op dance hall. A gang of us would go to the dances, it cost 2s to get in. Me and my friend Jean Downing went every week to the dances. We would do the waltz, ballroom, the Pally Glide and the barn dance. When the Yanks came over we used to say to them, 'Have you got any gum, chum?' We loved having them here, they were very generous. They would give us nylons, chocolate and gum.

Jean Beale

We danced all night

I was fourteen years old when I worked at Halls & Son at Stoke Golding. We made the socks for the Armed Forces. You had to start on other jobs and worked your way up to be a machinist. Me and my two friends used to bike to Witherley Hall to the dances that were on there. Displaced persons lodged at the Hall and they worked on the farms. They used to be at the dances and we used to really enjoy ourselves.

Mavis Turner

The sky was red and purple

My husband was given a one night leave from the Army because he was stationed at nearby Bramcote Barracks in Nuneaton. We went for a walk down Gypsy Lane. It was about ten o'clock at night when we could hear the bombs going off in Coventry. The sky was lit up in all colours, red and purple. I was working in munitions in Coventry and the next day when we were on the train we were told to get off at Foleshill . We walked all the way to Canley where the Standard factory was. You always wondered who you would or wouldn't see, every day that we went to work. I can remember the train being stopped at Exhall. There was an air raid on and some of the people dived underneath the train carriages to shelter. We were really late getting home but we still had to get up the next day and go to work, everyone did. I think most people were just glad to be alive and that's why you just got on with things. Everyone rallied around doing what they could when the war was on.

Phyllis Morris

The Land Army

New-found freedom

My father was a builder who was born in Wales. He met and married my mother in Birmingham. Mother worked in the Jewellery Quarter. I worked as a shorthand typist in an accounts office in Birmingham when the Second World War broke out. At the age of eighteen I wanted to join the ATS but my father forbid this and refused to sign my enlistment papers. Eventually I made the decision to join the Land Army without telling my parents. I forged my father's signature and felt very excited about leaving home and doing my bit for the war effort. My first placement was an old country house in between Evesham and Stratford-upon-Avon. It was a smashing place, the owner was a true gentleman. A Jewish girl, a Welsh girl and a local girl were the three girls I shared a room with – we all got on great. Mr Jones the foreman was a real character. He would tell us over and over again how the various farming jobs should be done until we

Right: Gwen Heath.

Below: Gwen Heath with her friend Lillie, in the WWAEC (Warwickshire Agriculture) truck.

got it perfect. German POWs were at the farm too. I worked with one German. I would lead the cart horse while he worked the plough. In the evenings dances were organised at the local Army camp. If it was after 11 p.m. when you got home the door would be locked. It was okay though if a roommate would leave the window open so that you could climb inside. One evening I landed in the ditch riding my bike – I did not realise how much the beer would affect me down at the local pub. It was a fantastic way of life; it was hard work but so much new-found freedom to enjoy – although our parents would not have approved of some of the antics we got up to! I went back to work as a typist after three years but I couldn't settle down. I decided to join up again as I missed the outdoor life so much. I was to be based in Atherstone, in a hostel on the Witherley Road. I was sent to work in the convent's gardens. The convent was situated in what is now Convent Close. I met a young man named Tony whilst working and living in Atherstone. We married and had two sons named Nick and Mark.

Gwen Heath

Best days of my life

They were the best days of my life. It was hard work at times. We learned all the various jobs on the farm like raking, hoeing, weeding, haymaking, mucking-out and milking the cows. Most of the other Land Army girls came from Yorkshire. I was lucky enough to live locally on the Watling Street at Grendon. The farm was owned by Mr and Mrs Fisher, they were a lovely couple. A week's wage was thirty shillings (£1.50) it does not sound much but every bit helped my mother. I wish you could turn the clock back, I really do. When I married my husband Reg, we rented a tied cottage, unfortunately it was demolished. Hopes of us living a life in the country were short-lived.

Joyce Reading

Joyce Reading tending the cattle at Fishers Farm, Grendon.

That night I lost my mom

We lived in Great Frances Street, Vauxhall, in Birmingham, but were bombed out one terrible evening when the bombing just would not stop. We were rehoused to Nechalls. Not long afterwards the bombing started all over again. My mom told me to take my younger brothers to the billiard hall where all the other children were and look after them. Mom and my older brother went to my gran's house, dad stayed at home. My gran's house was amongst the buildings caught in the blasts from the German bombs. Gran got buried underneath the rubble but luckily survived, my brother was severely burned. They carried a lady out who had been killed and needed someone to identify her. I volunteered and was sternly told, 'Oh no you won't'. A few moments later I was to find out it was my mom. My older brother who was burned badly went to live with gran. My brother, who was born profoundly deaf, stayed with my dad. My two other younger brothers were evacuated to Scunthorpe, where a couple named Mr and Mrs Bennett eventually adopted them both. We managed to keep in touch over the years, I made sure of that, I wrote to them both all the time.

I went to work in Aston in munitions; my work involved using the big Capston machines. Most of the men had gone to fight in the war so the work was left for women to do. The work made me feel ill so I decided I would join the Land Army. I was stationed at Oldberry near Henley-in-Arden where I did my training. I stayed at a very large house with other Land Army girls, which was situated three miles from the train station. It was a long walk to the station when we caught the train home at the weekend. After three months' training a lorry came to collect us and take some of us girls to Atherstone, a place we had never heard of. It seemed like we had been on the back of the lorry for hours. We eventually travelled through the town and the driver

Above: Ella Harrison.

Below: Ella Harrison (back left) with the friends she made in the Land Army.

shouted, 'We are here'. The hostel was on the Witherley Road where a beautiful willow tree stood at the front of the hostel, there is a house there now. I shouted to the driver, 'It's a strange place this is. There is only one long street! God made it, but he forgot to finish it'.

Being from the city, Atherstone was a little strange to begin with. I learned to ride a bicycle for the first time, supplied by the hostel. We went to work at various farms in the area. It was at Grendon Farm where I was to meet Ken. He worked at Baddesley pit but also helped out with the threshing at the farm. Ken helped to build the Ambulance Station at Grendon. We were only married for two weeks when he was called up to join the Royal Air Force. The hostel was burnt down after the war, I could not dare go and look. With so many memories of the bombing raids in Birmingham, I had seen enough fire, smoke and devastation to last me a lifetime. All this that's going on in the Gulf now, I watch our young lads on the television and think to myself, 'I hoped I would never live to see another war.'

Ella Harrison

Kiddle's farm

We all had our jobs to do – mum, dad, my brother Gordon, sisters Doris, Margaret, Jennifer and myself all worked long hours on the farm. The farmland was owned by Sir William Dugdale of Merevale Hall. During the war the government requested that farmers produce as much food as possible, rearing more livestock and growing more vegetables. Young girls joined the Land Army and were sent to farms all over the country. The Women's Land Army Hostel was in Mancetter. The girls would report to personnel from the Warwickshire Agricultural Executive Committee, based at Merevale Park POW camp, which was at the bottom of Merevale Park. Each day they would be given instructions as to where they would be sent to work. Early each morning the Land Army girls would turn up dressed in their brown and green uniforms and wearing wide-brimmed hats or scarves. There was Pamela from Birmingham, Bamba from Newcastle, along with half a dozen other girls. German and Italian POWs would arrive too, brought to the farm in lorries driven by soldiers based at the POW camp. Everyone worked from sunrise to sunset, my mother would bake something every day for them to eat at lunchtime. I was fourteen years of age at the time and on one occasion a bomb dropped into the yard at the farm. I remember diving under the kitchen table, thanking my lucky stars that it didn't explode. When Coventry was blitzed two families came to stay with us for two years. When the war ended they moved away, one family going to Hampshire. The Land Army girls returned to their home towns. Being a young lad I really missed them, especially Bamba.

Geoff Butler

The war effort needed the metal

They took all the iron fencing and railings from the houses in the town, to have it melted down for the munitions, but they didn't take the railings from the Old Bank House, the Council own it now. Years ago, when the war was on, a 'well to do' family lived there.

Ralph Fryer

Siren suits

People living down the bottom end of the town near the Cattle Arch would shelter under the hedges. The little children wore siren suits, an 'all-in-one' suit that zipped up to the neck. People would be there at all hours of the night. When the sirens went you just had to go, no matter what time it was.

Cynthia Fox

VJ celebrations in North Street, 1945. Second on the left is Sylvia Rose Burgess.

Air-raid shelters in Ratcliffe Road

The air-raid shelters nearest us were down Ratcliffe Road at the North Junior School. A bomb dropped near there once – my dad and his brother watched it come down.

Rita Deeming

I ain't looking, mate

I can remember my dad looking out through the window when the POWs were sweeping up the snow. My dad asked one of the soldiers if he could give the POWs a cigarette. The soldier said, 'I ain't looking, mate'. One day when the lorries and tanks came through the town, everyone ran out with hot drinks and food for the soldiers. My mother had baked a lovely cake for our Sunday tea. She took it outside and gave it to them. Very often lorries full of soldiers would stop, because Long Street was the main road through town in those days.

Dorothy Rushton

two

Housing and Agriculture

Take my suit to uncle's, son

I lived in the Phoenix yard in the 1930s. My dad, George, worked at Baddesley Colliery and my mother, Ena, trimmed hats at home. I had five brothers and sisters, Mona, George, Frank, Kathleen and Frances who died in infancy of TB and diphtheria. When I was old enough to ride a bike I got a job at Atherstone Hall where I collected the Bracebridge's washing, then take it to Merevale laundry in Meadow Street to be washed and pressed. I would sit in the hallway of Atherstone Hall and wait while the maid fetched me a bowl of hot soup to drink. I earned a shilling a week for taking the laundry and bringing it back. On Saturdays I would caddy for 10d a round, at the Atherstone golf course.

Money was short in those days. I remember every Monday my dad would tell me to take

The Prince of Wales, who later became King Edward VIII, passing Brown Bros pawnbrokers on Long Street in the 1930s.

F.J. Elliott's Tannery Works, Long Street (situated where Wainwright's garage now stands), c. 1920.

his suit to 'uncle's' and wait for the money! Uncle was the pawnbroker. I'd walk up the entry to a side door, where he would give me two shillings (10p) and a ticket to give my dad. My dad needed the money to get by on for the rest of the week. Every Friday on payday dad would give me two shillings and three pence and the ticket to get the suit back out from the pawnbroker's shop. On Monday I'd take the suit back again!

I left school at the age of fourteen and got a job at Elliott's Tannery. Me and Johnny Jones were playing 'Pitch and Toss' in the Tannery yard, it was a game played with the old pennies, we were having a great time when all of a sudden the foreman caught us and shouted that if we didn't get back to work we would get the sack. Work was work when I was a youth and there was no time for antics, you kept your head down and got on with your work. You only did something wrong once, at work or home, you wouldn't dare do it again, the discipline was tough. But I think it made real men of the youth in those days. I went to work down the pit at Baddesley and later on at Ansley pit. I was a miner for twenty-one years.

Bill Rowntree

Eveline Johnson, aged eighteen.

The baby in a shoebox

My cousin had a baby girl when she lived in the Phoenix yard. The baby only weighed one and a half pounds. She was so tiny that they kept her in a shoebox by the lead grate, she survived.

Eveline Johnson

We sang to Gilbert and Sullivan

There was a geyser bath at the top of our house, with a wooden seat in the bathroom, which got pleasantly warmed by the hot steam from the geyser. The bedrooms were cold unless lit with a coal fire, which only happened during illness. During a frosty spell there would be a beautiful pattern of ferns on the bedroom windows. Downstairs there was a fire in the kitchen range and sometimes I had a bath in front of this in a 'hip bath'. We would have a coal fire in the dining room and in the afternoon and evening there would be one in the drawing room as well. This room contained the piano which we gathered round for sing-songs from the Gilbert and Sullivan operas, and father played hymns on it on Sundays. There was no radio of course, so we were dependent on the piano and gramophone for music and for making our own entertainment.

Sylvia Rose Burgess

The Cotton Mill yard – 1920s

I often went to the Picturedrome with my dad; we called it the 'flea-pit'. There were times when you would come out scratching yourself where some bug had bitten you. It was exciting though as there were no televisions in those days and the silent movies were a thrill to go and watch. I can remember if the film broke down, we used to throw things till it came back on. My dad reared pigs in the yard. Once they were fattened up they were slaughtered. I remember hearing a pig squealing when my dad slit its throat. It was horrific, but it was a way of life in those days. I remember we had to hide a slaughtered pig when a local bobby was around. It was against the law to slaughter them by the houses.

The workhouse was opposite our yard, every day you would see the inmates walking in a group, supervised. I felt sorry for them. On Shrove Tuesday the ball used to be thrown over the wall so that they could have a kick. I remember seeing a man with a trolley, collecting a dead body from the workhouse, with just a blanket placed over the top of it. Some of us children went in the workhouse to collect jellies and cakes to take to the fête. The workhouse was demolished in the late 1930s and the Regal Cinema was built years afterwards. When the Regal opened, the queue stretched along Long Street right down to the Hollow where Wainwright's garage is.

Doris Holland

The Woolpack yard – 1920s

My mother and dad lived in the Woolpack yard, the houses were originally stables. They had twelve children altogether, seven and eight were twins and nine and ten were twins. My dad worked at the pit. Someone gave my mother a twin pram, they hadn't got much money in those days. My dad lost half of his

Anna Marie with seven of her twelve children, seen here in the Woolpack yard in 1930.

Anna Marie's first set of twins, in the pram which was given to her. Margaret is standing in the doorway, 1930s.

The Bonner girls enjoying their new council house in Bank Road in the 1940s.

finger when he was a youth working on the chaff cutter in the Woolpack yard. Some little kid turned it on while his finger was in it. The chaff cutter was used to cut the chaff for the horses. He had a bad squint as well, a bottle exploded in his face. The bottles used to have a little glass marble in the neck. It was great when we all moved into Bank Road in the 1940s – they were brand new houses that the council built.

Celestine Bonner

Times were very hard

My mother was Sarah Brown of the Cross Keys yard. She married George Clamp and they lived in Stratton Street. There was a big family, they didn't all survive, I was the youngest of about twelve children. Every Friday night was bath night. We all had a bath and our hair washed. Our clothes and underclothes were washed, aired and ready for the next re-clothing day. Times were very hard in those days.

Joyce Peart

Hallam's Square – 1940s

Hallam's Square was behind Shilton's shop and Gertie Hunt's shop in Long Street. There was an entry in between the two shops, which led into a square surrounded by little houses. The washhouse with a copper and a dolly tub and toilets were in the middle of the square. I can still visualise the tin baths, hanging on the outside wall. Washing lines hung from one side of the yard to the other. Mum tapped the windows every weekday morning to wake the neighbours up! Lil Cooper, Soldier Ford, May and Ernie Cope, Mrs Thomas, the

The Cross Keys yard, 1895. Sarah Elizabeth Brown (front left) is sitting with her mother. Sisters Charlotte, Alice Agnes and May Jane are standing.

Northall family and the Challis family lived in the square. There were steps leading from the square to Welcome Street. It was here that the coal was tipped up, we would collect it by the bucketful and put it in the coalhouse, which was just inside the houses where we lived. The houses were one up and one down. The walls were so thin you could see into next door's house where Ernie Cope lived and you could hear every sound. I slept on the landing with my younger sister Josie, as there was only one bedroom where my mam and dad slept.

We had a blacklead grate. On Fridays, mum would prepare corned beef stew in her dinner hour, then I'd put it on to cook, ready for us to eat when we all came home at about five o'clock. Some months of the year we would have pork, the pigs hung up in the yard on the meat hooks. If we were poorly with chickenpox or measles, my mam would tie brown paper around the light to stop the brightness because it was bad for your eyes.

My dad was killed at Baddesley pit in 1949, he was Luke Cheshire – one of the Cheshire lads who won the ball. My mam remarried Trainer Everitt. A few years later the council gave us a house in Kings Avenue, they were brand new. It was lovely moving into a new house, it seemed like a palace. My younger sister Beryl was born there.

Marilyn Smith

Aunt Beat's pet monkey

My aunt Beat, who was my dad's sister, lived at No. 204 Long Street, next to the Grammar School. It was a double house. The flats are there now. She and uncle Horace shared it with May and Ted Juggins, who had Phillip, Peter and Paul. My aunt Beat kept a monkey, she used to take him for a walk up and down Long Street, wearing his red jacket. She kept him tied up on the hearth, by the blackleaded grate. That was until we went up for tea! She

would invite us and then she let him off his lead, she did it every time. I was only a kid so it would have been about 1933. He used to jump on the table and pinch our food. He very often got out, but my aunt Beat would always find him down Church Walk.

Eveline Johnson

From rags to riches

My mother was Violet Shilton, whose parents owned Shilton's shop next to the Old Swan Inn in the 1930s. My dad, Tom Buckley, was a miner at Baddesley Colliery. My sisters Doll, Gladys, Joyce, Muriel, Margaret and Mary and my brother Dennis lived in a two up, two down house in Orton's yard. Orton's yard was opposite the train station by the White Hart Inn.

In the winter when it was cold and dark, we were scared to death because we had to carry a candle cupped in our hands hoping it would not go out. There was only two outside toilets and a washhouse to be shared by all the families. Each family had a specific time and day to use the washhouse. The women who had lived in the yard the longest sorted it, the longer you'd lived there the more say you had.

My mother made all our clothes out of hand-me-downs. I've seen my mother unstitch a coat, re-cut it and sew it up to make one to fit us. The buttons would be placed in one box, ribbons in another and different coloured fabrics unstitched and pressed and put in another box to use for something later. Even the smallest of pieces would serve a purpose for trimming the edges of a dress or something. The pieces from the old coats were used to make peg rugs. We had plenty of those all over the house. You would have to be really well off to have had a carpet in your house when we were kids.

Hilda Whelan

Orton's yard.

Wash day at granny's house

I can remember my granny (Edie Hall) telling me about her washdays. She had to light a fire under a stone copper that was in the washhouse, it was shared by the other women who lived in the yard. When the water was hot enough she used wooden tongues to put the washing in and out of the copper. The washing was scrubbed on a washboard with soap and a soft scrubbing brush. Then it would have to be soaked in clean buckets of water, ready for the mangle. The mangle had rollers where the washing was put through to remove the water from the clothes ready to hang out to dry. Sometimes the soot from the chimney fell into the water and she would have to start all over again.

Claire Neville

Swan with Two Nicks yard

I was born in the Swan with Two Nicks yard in 1920. I lived there till I was eight years old and then we moved to Stratton Street. In the Swan with Two Nicks yard we lived in a little house. I remember when the coal men brought the coal. We had to move the table first, so that they could get through the house and tip the coal under the stairs. The blackbats (beetles) used to come out and there were

Willday Terrace (Station Street end).

Cordingley Buildings.

The George & Dragon pub (now Gold & Silver Investments), Long Street, in the 1930s.

loads of them behind the pictures on the wall, we used to have to kill them. We had paraffin lamps in the house, there was no electric. At the end of our yard was Harry Boss, we used to get the paraffin off him. It was 3d for a quart, that's two pints. Victor Starr used to have a sale on every Friday at the George & Dragon, up the back yard. At the other end of our yard, over the wall, was Vero's factory.

Charlie Ross

The coaching house

I was born at No. 151 Long Street, a coaching house, in 1946. It used to be where the car park is opposite the job centre in Long Street. The house belonged to Mr Hiorns, who owned the pop factory in Meadow Street. Next door lived Mrs Mills, then there was Grubb's paper shop where Gladys Grubb worked, a small lady who wore hairgrips and always seemed

to be dressed in a brown coat. Maskell's sweet shop was on the other side, next to Mann's café, then came the Coach & Horses Inn. They were all demolished in the early 1970s. We had a Rhode Island Red cockerel. When we had to go to the toilet at the top of the yard, he didn't take any notice. But the minute we come out from the toilet to walk back to the house we had to run for it, he'd chase us and peck our ankles.

There were corn merchants and slaughter-houses at the end of the yards. There was a place called Skinner's yard opposite the Salvation Army hut in South Street where horses as well as cattle were skinned. My grandad worked for Sales & Son grinding the corn. My granny worked doing the washing and ironing for the Sales family and sewed the corn sacks with a 'great big needle'. Many a time the mice would jump out from the sacks when she was sat sewing them in the back yard.

Val Ford (left) with her dad, John Jurolec, standing in the front doorway of No. 151 Long Street.

Sidney Booton worked for Sale & Son until its closure in 1968. Sitting in the lorry is Roger Wood Snr.

Above: The canal-side view of the Silo Grain Mill in 1986. The Mill belonged to Kenneth Wilson.

Left: Sale & Son's Oast House, in Bonners yard, which was demolished to make way for the NWBC offices in South Street.

Sale & Son, South Street. Val Ford's granddad, Tom Ford, is seen here with other personnel in the 1930s.

At the coaching house lived Betty and Vicky Zeslowski. Two of their sons Eddie and John were born there. Next floor up lived my aunt Doll and uncle Bill. We lived on the top floor with my granny (Ada) and grandad (Tom), we were all related. When my mum was ill with diphtheria everything had to be sterilised and I had to sleep in a room at the very top of the house so that I wouldn't catch it. When the house was being demolished the builder found some groats (old English silver coins) in the same room where I'd slept. As far as I know they were handed to the Warwick Castle Treasury Department and put on display there.

Val Ford

Atherstone was a great little town

There were four cottages up our yard at the Hat & Beaver, I was born at the pub in 1918. George Thompson and his daughter Vera lived in one cottage. My grandad, Billy Deeming, and grandma, Sarah Ann Deeming, lived in the second one. My grandad Billy lit the gas lamps in Atherstone. He was the first lighter to ever do the job in the town. Billy was a tailor from Hatton. He came to Gopsall Hall near Twycross to be a tailor to Earl Howe in the 1800s before moving to Atherstone some years later. My uncle Fred Deeming (Piddy) lived in the third cottage, he won the Shrove Tuesday ball in 1910. Mr Bown from Dordon lived in the fourth cottage. Harry Garratt, the shoemaker and repairer, had a hut in Vinraces Row. Harry used to make the Shrove Tuesday ball every year. There were butchers, bakers, newsagents, fruit and veg shops, grocery stores, saddlers, corn exchange, Sandle's seed shop, haberdashers, cycle shop, garages, Hiscock's department store, Baxter's printers – where the *Atherstone News* was printed – Bert Webster's barbershop, furniture shops, crockery shops, Hall's carpenters and undertakers, Brown's pawnbrokers, Gem bus service and many more businesses trading and thriving in this small but very busy town. One of the main characters of that time was Sammy Southall, a magician who did sleight-of-hand tricks. His daughter Alice married a fairground worker who came with the Statutes fair one September.

Wilf Deeming

Milk round

I used to live in Gypsy Lane years ago. We had a milk cart and my younger sister used to come with me to fetch the milk from the Co-op in Nuneaton. We used to go around to all the houses with the milk cart and pour the milk into earthenware or glass containers.

We had jugs that measured a pint or half a pint. My dad's eldest brother would bike it all the way from Polesworth to feed the pigs. He didn't get paid in money, he had a pig instead, slaughtered for the table.

Ted Hatwell

Best black puddings in Atherstone

I can remember my mother telling me about Mr Frost of Frost's butchers. He made the best black puddings in Atherstone. They were only small but they were the best. He cooked them in a copper at the back of the yard and would get them out with a toasting fork. Then he would hang them up to cool down ready to sell to his customers. He had a few daughters,

Harriet and Walter Barlow, grandparents of Dorothy Walton and Beryl Gilliver, with their children Lizzie, Wal, Sam, Florence, George, Ted and the baby. The family lived in the Swan Entry, c. 1900.

Mr Frost did. I don't know whether there was three or four. They were lovely looking girls.

Dorothy Walton

The Druids Friendly Society

I remember my dad used to pay about a shilling a week to the Druids Friendly Society. At Christmas a party was put on for all the families who were members. There was no Welfare State in those days and people were proud. They didn't want charity if they could help it, so people joined these sorts of societies.

Mona Budge

Oddfellows

We made home-made remedies for illnesses and sickness. People couldn't afford to pay doctors' fees. We used to pay insurance to the Oddfellows Friendly Society in case we hit on hard times.

Beattie McCarthy

When the chickens crossed the road

We used to live in Vinraces Row in the '40s; it was a little yard with nine cottages, all one up one down, with a fairly big landing that could be used as a bedroom. Vinraces Row used to be attached to Denham and

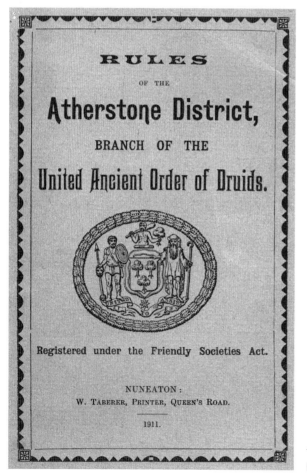

RULES

OF THE

Atherstone District,

BRANCH OF THE

United Ancient Order of Druids.

Registered under the Friendly Societies Act.

NUNEATON:
W. TABERER, PRINTER, QUEEN'S ROAD.

1911.

The Atherstone Druids Friendly Society handbook, 1911.

The Kings Arms yard.

Hargraves' buildings next door. Bert Webster's barbershop was on the other side of our entry. We had gardens in front of our houses and uncle Harry Garratt had his big shed where he made the Shrove Tuesday ball for years. Harry lost his leg in the First World War when he was just seventeen years old. Mr Wheatley had stables where he kept his horses and cart; he was the chimneysweep in the town. There was a slaughterhouse next to Mr Wheatleys. The gardens to the bank were next door, it's the HSBC bank now. It used to be the Midland Bank. Most of the yards in Long Street came out onto North Street on our side of the road. We were not far from the Hat & Beaver pub. Yards on the other side of Long Street came out onto South Street and Station Street. There were lots of allotments in Atherstone at one time, at the top end of North Street, down by the bungalow opposite the Cattle Arch, down Sheepy Road by the police station, up Coleshill Road, down Gypsy Lane and Holly Lane. There are still a few allotments about in the town but most of them were taken over for building on. There was one old chap called Belty Beaver who lived in another yard across the street. He had whiskers and dressed quite scruffy. We used to call him names and then make a run for it when he chased us back up the yard. I was always scrumping, there were lots of fruit trees everywhere. Down the bottom end of Long Street near The Clock, there would be chickens and fowl running about in the road. Some of the families kept them in the yards where they lived and they used to get out of the fowl pens.

Ralph Fryer

They came through town in their droves

When I was a young lad all the kids used to meet the farmers who came in the town with their droves of cattle and sheep on their way to the cattle market. They came through the town in all directions. All the kids would walk in front of the animals. The kids blocked off each entry along Long Street as they came to them to stop any of the animals getting up the yards, where they lived.

Joe Ford

I worked at Woolworth's

My mum used to make elderberry wine and once, I wasn't very old, I thought it tasted lovely and kept drinking it, I got drunk. My mum was Mabel Cook, granny Cook lived in Vinraces Row, there were two other sisters, Gertie who was the eldest and Daisy was the youngest, she was Ralph Fryer's mum. When I left school I got a job working at Woolworth's, I got £2 a week wages. I worked on the biscuit counter. They didn't sell them in packets then, they were weighed and sold by the pound and ounces. We had a Woolworth's for years in the town, it was a lovely shop.

Rita Deeming

The old tin bath

When we lived in Winters Terrace, my mum used to heat pans of water up on the blacklead grate to fill the tin bath up with hot water. The bath would be brought into the house from outside, where it was hung up. We used to get in the bath one after the other. Then we would get dry by the fire.

Jean Mills

Bill Haywood's farm

Bill Haywood's farm was in Gypsy Lane, just off the Sheepy Road. We used to walk

Ken Mills with Judy the dog in Winters Terrace (Frost's yard), c. 1953.

Cutting the winter oats, 1960. Geoff Butler is driving the tractor, whilst his dad Frances works the machine mechanisms behind the tractor.

down the lane, pushing our younger children in their prams and taking them with us to work in the fields. A cottage stood on the right-hand side just before you got to the farm. There was a big house on the corner, it stood in some lovely grounds. Bill Haywood's farm had a big gate, we went through the gate and made our way up to the barn and would sit on a trailer and wait for him. We ate our sandwiches on the trailer in the barn in the autumn and winter when the weather wasn't so good. There were other women who worked in the fields. Me and Gwen Johnson worked all the year around. We would start with the potato sorting, where the potatoes had been stored through the winter months in the barns. Then we would set them sitting

on the back of the trailer, while Mr Haywood made the holes with a machine up and down the fields. We did the same with other plants such as cabbages. He would ring a bell when it was time to drop in the potatoes or plants. This way the plants would grow in perfect rows, spaced out correctly. We did mangel chopping, the mangels weren't for humans to eat, they were planted for animal food. We did hoeing and pea picking as well. In fact there was lots of work to do at the farm. The older children came during their school holidays. They seemed to enjoy the freedom of playing in the fields. Sometimes they helped us pick the potatoes. A gentleman farmer from Sutton wanted us to work for him for a few weeks. There was me, Gwen Johnson and two other women. He fetched us in his great big car. We worked for a farmer called Mr Coley once, in Holly Lane. He still used to work the fields the old-fashioned way – he had two cart horses that pulled the plough up and down the rows.

Beryl Freeman

The last and final bit

It was an ice-cold, frosty morning, me and Beryl were working in the small field behind the cemetery. It was freezing and nasty. 'Let's get the job done and then we can go home',we said to each other. I swear there must have been six mangels at a time in the air, we were chopping them so fast. We sweated our guts out to get finished. It should have taken us all day to finish, there was a day's work, but we did it by dinnertime. Do you know what – he only paid us for half a day! Do you know why we had to work in the fields? To supplement the poor wages of the men. We took the children to work with us until they were old enough to go to school.

Gwen Johnson

three

Childhood and Schooldays

My childhood 1914-24

There was a long garden attached to Irvine House, running from Long Street to North Street where we played hide and seek, i-i-kee, whip and top, hopscotch, skipping, marbles, and tennis and croquet on the lawn. In winter children would play skipping in the street, in the lamplight when it was evening. I would play various letter games with my brothers and so I was able to read before I went to school. Occasionally we would visit the local cinema housed in the old Corn Exchange and nicknamed 'the cornic'. Here we laughed at the antics of Charlie Chaplin and wept silently at the pathos of Jackie Coogan. At one end of Long Street was the dreaded workhouse, where old people went if their children had no room for them. Couples were callously separated. Tramps might also lodge there for the night, but had to chop wood to pay for their board. The railway station was at the other end of the street. We were friends of the stationmaster and once, when there were no trains running on Boxing Day, we went to a party and dance in the waiting room where there was a huge coal fire in the grate. This was one of many parties at Christmas, with charades always being popular, especially if you could dress up. The shops were decorated only a week or so before Christmas with tinsel and strands of cotton, and the sweet shops displayed pink sugar mice and chocolate Father Christmas figures. Children hung their stockings up as now, but the most they would contain would be an orange, nuts and raisins and I would be very pleased if I was given a book for Christmas, as there was no children's library in Atherstone. I remember being given *Arabian Nights*, *The Water Babies* and *Alice in Wonderland*. Apart from these books, I had perforce to read my brothers' books over and over again – *Deerfoot on the Prairies*, *Robin Hood*, *Tales of King Arthur* and also to devour their weekly magazine, the *Boy's Own Magazine*. I was allowed *The Children's Newspaper* and the comic *Rainbow*, *Grimm's Fairy Tales* and Hans Christian Andersen. When small, my father recited the dramatic Old Testament stories of Abraham and Isaac, Noah, Joseph and his brothers, Daniel in the lion's den, David and Goliath and fiery furnace.

If there was snow and frost during the winter months my brothers would take me tobogganing up the Outwoods and skating on Sheepy Pool or Oldbury Reservoir. In the summer months we went for walks on the Outwoods, where there were grand places for picnics, or to the bluebell woods, which appeared like a sea of blue during late April and May. Sometimes we walked on to Oldbury Reservoir, where we bathed, there being no public swimming baths then in Atherstone. We also cycled to Twycross Woods to pick primroses, violets in the hedgerows and cowslips in a field between Ratcliffe and Sibson. On bank holidays we would always visit a farmer friend to see his animals and, if wet, to eat our picnic in his barn on his bales of straw and probably have tea in the farmhouse kitchen. He always brought a sheaf of corn to decorate the Wesleyan church at harvest time when there was a Harvest Thanksgiving service and a Harvest Supper on Monday evening. The children's gifts were taken to the sick or elderly members of the congregation. Occasionally, there would be a magic lantern show at the church (or chapel as it was called then) and other social evenings such as concerts in which the children took part. There was a Christmas party for the Sunday school children, with the customary fare – red and yellow jellies, fish paste or sardine sandwiches, blancmange and bought cakes, and games like Blind Man's Bluff, and Musical Chairs, Pass the Parcel, I Wrote a Letter to My Love, Trencher and Oranges and Lemons.

Sylvia Rose Burgess

The May Queen

On 2 May, schoolchildren often danced around a maypole and the May Queen, chosen by Mancetter schoolchildren, was crowned on the village green. One year, I remember they danced all the way down Church Walk. On the 29 May children had to be sure to wear oak leaves, if possible, as it was 'Royal Oak Day', when boys might otherwise hit our bare legs with stinging nettles.

Sylvia Rose Burgess

When the 'bob' was the fashion

After the First World War it was fashionable for children's long hair to be cut short and so mine was bobbed, as it was then called. I would be dressed in the winter in 'combinations', long woollen stockings, liberty bodice which had to be buttoned for me at the back, navy serge dress or navy kilt and red jumper, with a blue velvet dress for Sundays and for wearing at parties. If muddy I wore boots and brown gaiters, which buttoned up at the side with a buttonhook. My coat, I remember, was a heavy navy blue one and I wore a sailor hat, which had 'HMS *Renown*' on its ribbon.

Sylvia Rose Burgess

We thought we'd got the moon

I went to the Infants' School that was on the corner of North Street. The headmistress was Miss Harrison, if I remember right! We used to have a black slate board and chalk to write with and an abacus with coloured beads on to learn to add up. I'm going back eighty-three years you know. Happy days they were you know, happy days. We didn't answer back, not like they do today, you wouldn't dream of it. We always respected the teachers and would say 'Yes, Miss' or 'No, Miss', not call them by their Christian name. I think it was better years ago; today the mums are all out working. When we got home there was always someone there. My mother died when I was five years old so I can't remember exactly who got me from school. I do remember my auntie stepped in to help the family. My younger brother Jack went to live with her. My dad had a housekeeper. Jack wasn't very old when my mother died, me and my older brother stayed at home with my dad.

You could get a ha'p'orth of sweets or a penn'orth of sweets. These days they want a pound don't they! I never went to the seaside until I left school. Sunday school was great with the treats, we had to take our own cup. We followed the Marching Band all around the town until we got to the place where we were to spend the day: the grounds of Atherstone Hall, where the Bracebridges lived. We thought we'd got the moon when we got to the tea party, we were so happy.

Mary Fox

The Atherstone Infants' School building in North Street. The building, seen here in 2004, is now the Rowan Centre.

Atherstone infants group, 1932. Gerald Eaton is centre back.

Standing on the steps of Athersone Infants' School in 1947 are, from left to right, Mrs Welford, Mrs Douglas, Mrs Goodridge, Nancy Crawley-Bouvey (headteacher), Mrs Tucker, Mrs Gooding and Mrs Filo. Dorothy Rushton is sitting.

Those were the days, my friends

The rag and bone man lived in the next yard to us. He would pay us halfpenny for a small jam jar and a whole penny for a large jam jar or a rabbit skin. After he had paid us we would scrump his apples and pears then run. The yards would have lots of children living in them. They had big families in them days. We would all play together, hopscotch, whip and top and outing. Outing was our favourite game and we would split into two gangs – one would hide while the others had to find them. We had fun annoying people too, by pinning a button on a letterbox and pulling the cotton through to make a tapping noise. We thought it was hilarious when they opened the door and no-one was there. When it snowed my dad would organise snowball fights between the children from the other yards. He would organise ball games in the summer months. There were hundreds of children living in Long Street before the yards were demolished. Although there wasn't a lot of money around, people helped each other. Children would run errands and be rewarded by a few pennies or a bag of sweets. We always shared them out with our brothers and sisters, you never kept anything just for yourself. Every school day at twelve o'clock I had to collect my teacher Miss Barnsley's dinner from Mr Barnsley (her brother) who owned the wool shop. Then I had to take it to her before I went home for my dinner! At Christmas time we would go carol singing at the big house down the road, where Mr and Mrs Vero lived. We would be invited inside to sing to the family and their guests, it was lovely, but we felt a bit shy, singing in front of everyone. We did enjoy the treats though, they gave us biscuits, cake and a glass of lemonade. A real luxury in those days!

Hilda Whelan

They called it discipline

I went to St Benedict's School in Owen Street. Not the school at the end of Owen Street, the one next to the chapel, the chapel is still there. You went when you were five years old and stayed there until you left school at fourteen years old. You didn't go to another school, just that one. Mrs Bakey, Miss Murray, Mrs McCauliff and Mrs Wilson were teachers. The cane was across the teacher's desk all day long, ready for when you stepped out of line. I had a few doses of it, the same as everyone else did. You had to hold your hand out. They called it discipline. The headmistress caned us if the teacher sent you to her.

Bill Rowntree

'Fest I Lent'

I went to the Infants' School in 1930, Miss Harrison was the headmistress and Mrs Smart, Miss Pratt and Miss Berry were the teachers. Then I went to Parries School, that's what we called it then, the school next door to the infants – the North Junior School. Miss Crowl was the headmistress and Connie Barnsley was

Milly Evans at Atherstone Senior School, 1928.

Nancy Lees at Atherstone Senior School, 1950.

my teacher. We used to get the ruler across our fingers if we did anything wrong. After that I went to the senior school, they call it Queen Elizabeth Lower now don't they? Mr Guy was the headmaster; there were two Miss Neales, who were sisters – Dorothy and Daisy. Miss Wheeler, Mr Sanders, Mr Rollason, Mr Macnamara were teachers and Miss Hamlet and Miss Thomas were both cookery teachers. I loved assembly in the school hall, we sang hymns every day, my favourite hymn went: 'Glad that I live am I that the sky is blue/ Glad for the country lanes and the fall of dew/ After the sun the rain, after the rain the sun/ This is the way of life, that the work be done'. We used to wear different coloured sashes you know – green for Bourne, blue for Bracebridge, yellow for Sale and red for Allen, after the names of the big men in the town. Mr Guy used to stand outside the classroom looking in to us with his hands behind his back. That's when you knew he was there. That's when you had discipline. We had respect then. If you were sent outside the class to stand in the corridor, you were waiting for punishment and if Mr Guy came along he sent you to his office and would cane you. Mr Sanders threw chalk at you if you weren't concentrating. We called him Bonzo, he was a devil, we were all frightened of him. We used to wear gymslips, a school hat like Deanna Durban used to wear in navy blue with our school badge on it, the Bear with the Rugged Staff representing Warwickshire. In the first year it was First Year 1, First Year 2, First Year 3, and then it would go Second Year 1, Second Year 2, Second Year 3, then Third Year 1, Third Year 2, Third Year 3, and so on. Miss Furness read us the *Jungle Book* by Rudyard Kipling at senior school, she was our PT teacher, but she read the book all the way through for us. She was lovely, when we left school we got her autograph and she signed her name with the words 'Fest I Lent'. I wish I knew what it meant. Someone once said it was Latin, I would love to find out.

Dorothy Walton

School dinners in the Town Hall

When we were at the Infants' School, we used to have to walk to the Town Hall for our dinners. We had to all walk in a line under the archway everyday, by the old doctor's surgery under the Swan entry to the market place. When I started senior school I rarely stayed, once I got my mark on the register I would clear off for the day down Levies Farm. I spent most of the time lassoing the cows and messing about. The fields used to come right up to the town in those days, the housing estates weren't there then. One of the fields was called 'The Sand Holes', it was used for rabbiting.

Ralph Fryer

Senior School boys, 1932/33. From left to right: Mr Guy, W. Benford, ? Callis, R. Sketchley, Mr McManners, -?-, ? Thumbwood, ? Ward, J. Brown, W. Tweed, -?- , -?- , J. Pratt, -?-.

Senior School girls, 1932/33. From left to right, back row: Miss Thomas, Ada Goodwin, Eileen Barratt, Kathleen Stokes, Miss Duffield. Front row: Edith Daft, Dorothy Newitt, Beryl Bircher, ? Hargreaves, D. Horton.

Old-fashioned dinner

I was the meat cook at Atherstone High School in the 1960s. The kitchens are now demolished. We cooked for another eight schools as well. Newton Regis was one, Herbert Fowler School was another, I can't remember what the others were. 5s a week the dinner money was then, that's about 25p today. 5s was what the children paid for years, 1s a day for a lovely old-fashioned dinner and pudding. They were beautiful dinners, well we thought so anyway. What do they have now?

Beryl Gilliver

I was a nursery nurse

I worked under Nancy Crawley-Bouvey for a couple of years, at the old Infants' School. I used to help Nancy at Sunday school, that's how she came to ask me if I wanted to help out at the Infants' School. I started college in March 1948 and was there for two and a half years. My training included going to residential nursery schools, nursery schools in Rugby, Shirley and Stratford-upon-Avon. When I had finished my training, I took my college exam and the national exam for NNEB. I worked at a nursery in Nuneaton for a while. Later I accepted a job at Atherstone Nursery and worked under Veronica Welford. Veronica was the headmistress at the time. The nursery was specially built by Social Services as a day nursery for working mothers during the Second World War. It was governed by a matron then. The babies and children stayed all day. They had their lunch and slept in the afternoons on little beds. Veronica Welford worked under Warwickshire County

Above: Children play on the apparatus at nursery school in 1951 while Dorothy Rushton supervises.

Left: Gary Fulleylove, Tony Foster and Christine Freeman are the three children sitting on the middle row. Maureen Johnson is sitting (front right), 1957.

Council Education Department. There was Miss Dunning who was a teacher, Joyce Dando who was a Nursery Nurse and myself working there in 1948. I worked at the nursery for twenty years before I left to have my son. When I returned to the nursery, I stayed until I retired, in 1993. Mrs Ann Clay was the headmistress at that time. I had worked there for over forty years. There were many changes over the years. It went from an all-day nursery, to a morning and afternoon nursery. The beds had all gone, as they weren't needed anymore. We organised lots of trips to places like Whipsnade Zoo and local farms. The trips were organised to combine fun with education for the children. We hired local buses from De-Luxe Coaches. Parents came as well on the trips. We had a Parents and Teachers Association, where we would all fundraise, to meet the costs of the children's Christmas parties. We held Beetle-Drives and Rummage Sales etc. Every year we had the maypole out, for the children to dance around on May Day. I have so many lovely memories. I have met some lovely people and children through my work. I always knew that I wanted to work with children. I wouldn't change it for all the tea in China.

Dorothy Rushton

Things were taboo

When I was at school in the late '40s, there were a lot of things that were taboo. There

Gordon Gudger driving the 'motor car' built for him by his dad, complete with tax disc, outside No. 11 Garden Row, c. 1930.

were things you didn't talk about or dare ask about. You couldn't even draw cow's teats on a picture that you drew! You think I'm joking don't you? Honest it's true.

Ralph Fryer

Davy Crockett, king of the wild frontier

When we lived at Merevale Park, in the prefabs that were built during the war, there was a big water tower at the camp and in the hot weather we would climb up and play in the water. It was about 1956. All the lads had a Davy Crockett hat because we were all Davy Crockett mad at the time. They were fur hats with a 'tail' at the

back. We sang 'Davy, Davy Crockett, king of the wild frontier' all the time.

Horace Doherty

Tiger Moth crash

I was thirteen years of age at the time. There were three of us; Tom Dunn, Ken Russell (Rusty) and myself. We were sledging up the Outwoods on a Saturday afternoon when suddenly there was a terrific snow blizzard. We could hear the sound of an aeroplane, labouring in the not too far distance. There was a sudden silence, then a whooshing noise and the sound of branches breaking. Unsure

Peter Doherty, uncle Ernie and Horace Doherty outside their prefab at Merevale Park, 1953.

of what was happening, we returned home, going our separate ways. The snow blizzard was getting worse by the minute, we could hardly see before us. I made my way back home to the Outwoods farm and my two friends lived up the lane, past the toll cottage that was situated on the corner of the road going up to Ridge Lane. When I arrived home my mother explained that there had been a plane crash. I soon realised that that was the noise we had all heard up the Outwoods. My two friends, Tom and Ken, actually saw the pilot hanging from a tree by the toll cottage, with his parachute tangled up. He was a Canadian pilot who was on a training exercise from nearby Bramcote Barracks at Nuneaton – flying a Tiger Moth aeroplane! Tom and Ken had helped him down, the pilot wrapped the parachute up and asked where the nearest telephone was. Luckily, Tom Dunns father had a telephone at nearby Bentley Cottage. The pilot had to report to base and explain what had happened. He had attempted to follow the train line route, but visibility was impossible, which caused the plane to crash into the woods behind the Beehive Cottage.

Sunday morning came, I called at Ken Russell's house, he had occasion to take something to Mr and Mrs Heath who lived at the Beehive Cottage. As we arrived we were greeted by a guardian, dressed in Air Force blue. He'd been sent to guard the wreckage of the Tiger Moth aeroplane that had crashed on the side of the lake and was lodging at the Beehive whilst on his mission.

Keith Reynolds

Collecting autographs

We used to go to the back of the Red Lion and wait to see if we could get the autograph from a celebrity who would be staying there. There was a lot of famous people who stayed at the Red Lion over the years. I can remember Victor Sylvester, he used to come with his band and a coach full of people and stay at the Red Lion. There used to be a lot of coaches parked outside at one time.

Jean Mills

The 'Flea Tree'

I started Atherstone North Junior School in 1961, our teacher was Miss Sharrott. At the back of the classroom was a tray with little white inkpots, with a small enamel jug with a long thin spout. The jug was full of ink and it was my job as one of the classroom monitors to fill the inkpots and give them out to the rest of the class. Our desks had a hole in where the inkpot fitted inside. The pens were wooden with a nib at the end. When we wrote with the nib pens we had to press blotting paper over the writing to dry the ink. We used to get ink all over our fingers. The next year we were allowed to use biros, which the school supplied. There was a tree in the playground called the 'Flea Tree'. If you came last in a game, the forfeit was that you were held around the 'Flea Tree'. We would pull the kids arms around the tree and tease them that they had got fleas. We had to learn about ten new spellings every day. I've always said it was Mrs Hall, our teacher, who I owed for being a good speller. If you talked in class you got lines to do – 'I must not talk in class'. In fact if you did anything wrong you got lines to do as a punishment. I remember getting the slipper off the headmaster once. I can't remember what for but I think it was a trivial thing at the time. My teacher was upset with me about something and he sent me to the headmaster. I was in the third year at that time. When we did our school play I always volunteered to play a part. I loved to be in the school play.

When I started Atherstone High School I was amazed because the teachers who had a reputation for being very strict were really great. They were never a problem, perhaps this was because they were strict, but fair too. We girls had to learn cookery and needlework, while the lads learned metalwork, woodwork and gardening. The woodwork teacher had a blackboard rubber called 'Black Jack,' he threw it at the lads if they misbehaved. When we were in the third year a new subject was introduced, it was called Humanities. It was a trial subject and our class was the first to study it, a kind of experimental study, Mr Wes Hall was our teacher, it was so different to Maths and English, where we would have to sit with our heads down in our books, concentrating on our schoolwork. It was the first time that we actually had discussions with a teacher and was able to share our thoughts and feelings about world issues in a group. Was this the start of children being heard? I don't know!

There were times for practical jokes – you weren't a kid if you didn't mess about. Once when we were in our needlework class, we were trying on our school dresses that we'd made. There was a big wardrobe in the classroom. We pulled the screen around the wardrobe and two of us got inside it. One of the other girls pulled the screen away. The teacher wondered where we were, we couldn't stop laughing. We did the 'disappearing' trick about three times. She was a lovely teacher, Mrs Walker was her name. She never said a word to us about it. In Biology we always sat at the back of the class. Then we could let the white mice out of the cage and play with them. We used to put them up the sleeves of our jumpers, while we were doing our writing!

Christine Freeman

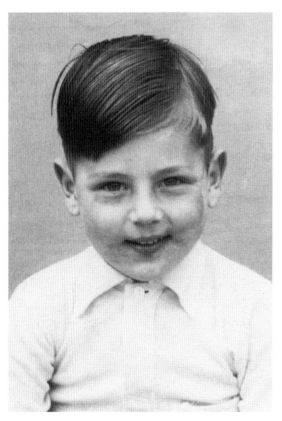

Malcolm Freeman, 1953.

Boat ride back from school

When we lived at Merevale Park, from 1952 to 1957, me and our John went to South Street Junior School. We moved there from the Coach and Horses yard, where we had lived for about two years. When school time was over we would go to the top lock on the canal and ask the boat people for a lift down to the Kings Head, we thought it was great. I remember the great big bonfires at the camp. All the miners would split the fallen trees in half and stand them up, to make the biggest bonfire.

Malc Freeman

Goodbye, children, goodbye

I loved school, especially Atherstone Infants' School and the North Junior School – although I remember Miss Tempest used to sit at a big desk and if you were naughty she would hit you across your knuckles with her ruler! As for Atherstone High School, it wasn't so good. I think it was because we all went through our first years of school together, up to the age of twelve years. Then when we got to the High School there were other kids from Mancetter, Grendon and Baddesley. Most of us went into different classes and different coloured house groups. Our large group that went through school together were now being split up. We lost that closeness that we had all grown up together with. Funny thing now is that we have all done a full circle, reached fifty and talk about those school years.

My mum made the fairy dresses for the Junior School Pandemonium in 1964. She sewed sequins on all the dresses. Mum made the white yokes for the Infants' School choir so that we all looked nice for the Harvest Festival. I remember one of the teachers being knocked over by some of the lads. They were running about and as she fell, her legs went up in the air and we could see her big blue bloomers. When she told us to put the tables down after our sewing class, which was in the dinner hall, we would only put one side of the trestle legs down, then we could slide down on the tabletops. Every time we did this, until she shouted at us. In the playground at Infants' School Miss Crawley-Bouvey (the headmistress) used to play the accordion and we would dance and sing 'Here we go round the mountain two by two/ Show us a little action two by two'. We all had to stand in a line, holding hands with a friend. Then walk across the playground, down the steps, passed the Congregational chapel and into a small building which was shaped like a Nissen Hut. This is where we had our dinner. It was a peculiar building. I wish I knew what it was originally. There were gravestones by the side of it. We had our Christmas parties upstairs in the chapel. We used to sing 'Soldier, soldier, won't you marry me, with your musket, fife and drum?', and the boys would sing back to the girls 'No sweet maid I cannot marry you, for I have no hat to put on!' We'd sing it until the soldier finally sang at the end, 'I've a wife and a baby at home!' When we left the Infants' School, everyone would sit on the floor in the upstairs room of the chapel. All of us who were leaving had to sing to all the other children we were leaving behind 'Goodbye, children, goodbye/ Goodbye, children, goodbye/ We'll see you again, but we don't know when/ Goodbye, children, goodbye.'

Valda Deeming

The New Estate

The New Estate was what the locals called it. In 1957 new houses had been built, namely Lister Road, Tudor Crescent, Friary Road, St Georges Road and Mythe View. Young couples with families had been rehoused from other areas of the town, such as the yards. My own family along with other families had been

Above: Atherstone Hall prior to demolition, 1964.

Left: Humanitarian and friend of the famous Florence Nightingale, Charles Holte Bracebridge of Atherstone Hall, 1799-1872.

rehoused from Merevale Park, previously the POW camp. In Tudor Crescent alone, there were ten of us in the same class at Infants' School.

Our sports days were held in the Atherstone Hall grounds. The girls took part in the egg and spoon race, whilst the boys took part in the sack race. I remember well the nature walks with Mrs Perrin, our teacher at the Infants' School. Daffodils and crocuses looked lovely in the spring. The autumn came and we collected different types and coloured leaves. Various organisations held their garden fêtes in the grounds of Atherstone Hall. 1964 came and the Big White House, as we called it, was demolished. The green pastures that we once played on, took picnics, made daisy chains, and were forever looking for four leaf clovers to bring us luck, was now being dug up by earth diggers to make way for the new A5 bypass.

The hedges where the older lads had made dens and took old armchairs to sit on were being ripped up. Heaps of dirt, diggers and lorries took over this once beautiful ground. As a child we would sit on the back of the workman's small truck and pretend we were in a carnival – it was great fun. The boys off our estate and the boys from Kings Avenue and Bank Road had cone fights, throwing them at each other behind the mounds of dirt.

The winter of 1963 was one of the worst ever, but it didn't stop us having fun. The bypass froze over; we would skate on the ice and make slides. I remember my foot going through the ice, taking my Wellington off – wringing my sock then going back to make more slides. Others fell through the ice from head to foot! Somehow nobody seemed bothered about how cold it was.

Christine Freeman

The pastures being dug up to make way for the A5 bypass through Atherstone in 1963. Friary Road is on the left of the photograph. The mass of trees on the far right was the Atherstone Hall grounds.

Dirt diggers and cranes in the same vicinity. Creating new pathways from the Sheepy Road housing estate, 1963.

Pulling your leg

We were living in Tudor Crescent, there was Henry, Sammy, Butch, Ann, Carol and our Susan was a baby. When the bypass was being dug out, there was a big park with a big white house in the middle, like a stately home. It was eerie when it was standing empty, when there was no one living in it, we used to think it was haunted. Cobby Webster was the leader of the gang, we used to knock about with him. One night we got over the wall that went all the way around the outside of the park, and was about six feet high. We went inside the house and it smelt fusty, it was horrible. We had no torches, you couldn't afford things like that, we took a box of matches. We made our way down some steps in the house, being kids we thought there were dungeons down these steps. There were chains and all sorts of rubble and stuff. In the rubble something was sticking out, it was a wooden leg. We were frightened to death but we hung onto it. We ran all the way back to the estate, god knows what we were going to do with this leg. Anyway, someone, I can't remember who, suggested that we put a sock, shoe and a trouser leg on it. It was the summer holiday, so we were using our imagination a bit. Where they were digging up the bypass they were making a sloping path to go up to the side of the other road. There were dirt tracks off the estate at that time, under this sloping path was a bit of a tunnel, with bricks and rubble lying about. The next day we decided we would go and bury the leg under a few bricks and rubble, so that it was sticking out, and hide in the other side of the tunnel. 'Quick there's someone coming, there's someone coming.' Just like today, some people walked past and took no notice. But you got the odd woman who would try to shift the leg and say something like 'I'll get an ambulance', or 'phone the police'. Then we had to make a run for it, we didn't want to get in trouble with the police. This one time we were there again, waiting for someone to walk past. 'Help, help me', we murmured, this chap stopped and started saying, 'Don't you worry me man, just you wait a bit, I'll get you out'. He started to move the bricks, then he grabbed the leg and we all jumped up and ran off, we didn't see his face, we were busy getting away from him. He had the leg, swinging it at us as he chased us down the road shouting 'I'll kill you if I get my hands on you'.

Steve Owen

Was it a medieval cemetery?
When me and my dad used to go and watch the Adders at the football ground, we used to take a shortcut through the park at Atherstone Hall. There were two lodges on Ratcliffe Road, Mr and Mrs Douglas lived in one of them. That was the entrance we walked through, it brought us out on the Sheepy Road, near the Stable Block – the council yard is there now. When I was a fireman we used to have fire practice in Atherstone Hall, before it was demolished. Someone found an old map one day. It was a really old map, with the words 'Blood Bank' written on it. We had reason to believe that this is where the bodies from the Battle of Bosworth were buried, in a mass grave. The 'Blood Bank' we thought, according to the map, was likely to be a medieval cemetery. I don't know what happened to the map, it was very old.

George Blower

See-saw, compliments of the builders
Remember the big empty steel oil drums that the builders used to leave lying around? We would put a plank across the steel drum and make a see-saw. All the kids did that then didn't they? I was sitting on one end of the plank one day when a few lads jumped on the other end. I was catapulted into the air and I smashed my elbow, the bone came straight through my arm. That was a trip to the hospital that day.

There was a timber yard where Croft Road is now, allotments just down the road where the police station is now. There was a big house with an orchard where we went scrumping for apples over the wall. It was near where the swimming baths are now. We went to play inside the house when it was empty, our Ann was there and Gaz Jackson. The ceiling collapsed and our Ann got trapped under the rubble. Gaz had a brick hit him on the head. There were lots of old buildings being pulled down in the area. There were lots of new ones being built as well. That's what the kids did, played where the builders were working.

Steve Owen

The bathing bridge
I can't be sure of the year but it was around 1947. The summer was hot and we kids had to sit it out in a stuffy unfriendly classroom most of the day. Come four o'clock we could not get away from the school fast enough. It was like a stampede to escape the teachers, who I thought were horrid. On the way home my pals were talking about going swimming later that evening. There were no public baths in the area in those days so I asked them where they were going, 'Up the canal, by the bathing bridge'. The bathing bridge was near the field at the lower end of the Outwoods, near Westwood Road. I wouldn't ask my mum and dad if I could go, I knew they would say no, although I remember them going in when I was younger. A case of do as I say, not what I do! I had done all my nightly chores that I had to do, I always had some sort of work

to do after school finished. Being as quiet as possible I found a pair of the old chap's swimming trunks. I snuck out the back door and ran to the Bathing Bridge as fast as my legs could take me. Fred Baddeley and Nancy Morris were there, I can't remember who the others were now. Fred asked me if I could swim and when I told him no, him and his mate grabbed me by my arms and ankles and threw me into the Cut. This was the way I learned to swim, in the Cut like a lot of other kids did. The canal wasn't too deep then, it had been said that one of Samuel Barlow's coal barges had overturned, spilling its entire load of coal. Consequently the depth of the water was halved. Samuel Barlow's barges were used a lot for transporting coal southwards, along the canal. Someone grassed on me to my parents about my swimming, probably some grown-up. The place was infested with grown-ups. Just waiting to tell your parents if you did anything you shouldn't be doing. They appeared to get their entertainment that way, getting kids in trouble. The police got involved and people stopped going, I suppose we never saw the dangers, being kids.

Keith Reynolds

Penny bangers

We used to go down the lanes past the Alder Mill and go conkering. We would climb the trees and shake loads of conkers off the trees. We made the hole with a meat skewer and threaded a lace through them, sometimes we baked them to try and make them tougher. Near Christmas we collected chestnuts by the sackful and roasted them in the open fire

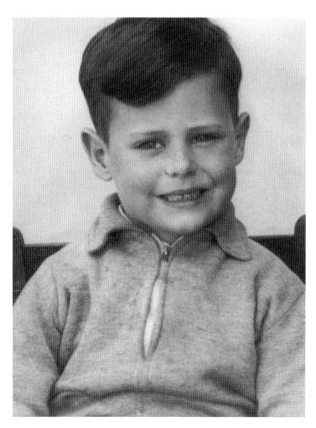

John Freeman, 1953.

when we got back home. We played marbles in the streets and ended up with pockets full of them. All the lads used to make bows and arrows with a thick branch, sharpened with our penknives to a point. The flights were made out of two playing cards, usually the picture ones because they looked better. A gang of us used to go trainspotting at the train station, we used to sit on the wall or wait on the railway bridge. As soon as the green light came on in the signal box, you knew it wouldn't be long before a train came along. Me, our Malc, Dave Pattinson, Joey Cheshire, Mick Taylor and loads of other lads used to go.

We were always asking the mums for the wheels off their old prams. The old-fashioned pram wheels were great for the trolleys that we made out of wood, a nut and bolt, and a length of string, they were like go-carts. We could steer them with the string, our feet each side of the wheels. We used to go camping in the fields and make a campfire, we only had a two-man tent, but we thought it was great.

Bonfire night was really good, we spent weeks getting loads of rubbish and wood off everyone. People had the bonfires in their back gardens then. Almost everyone had a bonfire, it was a good excuse to burn the old settees, tables and beds that people didn't want. We always slit the settees or chairs open first and tipped them up, just in case there was any money inside them, before it went on the bonfire. You never knew how much loose change you were going to find. The bonfires would burn all night. Jumping Jacks, Catherine Wheels and Rockets were good. We liked to buy the penny bangers with our paper round money and let them off. We had a paper round and took the *Tribune* in the week and the Pink *Tribune* on a Saturday. The Pink had all the sporting news in it. On Friday night we had to collect the money from all the customers we had delivered to. It was great if

you got tips, most of them did tip you, a load of 3d tips mounted up. Can you remember the old threepenny bits? They were little brass twelve-sided coins.

John Freeman

Woodbines were 'two a penny'

We used to collect the empty fag packets. There was me, Jimmy Dunn, Pete Martin, Bozzer Bolls and Joey Wall. Woodbine and Craven 'A' packets were two a penny. We used to look for the Lucky Strike packets and other brands. We walked up the Watling and Merevale Lane. I can remember when we walked up Merevale Lane, that was the first time I'd ever been to Baddesley. We ended up right up at the Folly.

David Russell

I loved the day trips

I remember the day trips to the seaside with the Legion and the Football Club. We went to Blackpool, Rhyl and Weston-Super-Mare. They gave all the kids 10s each and packets of crisps and a bottle of pop on the bus going. We all had pop and crisps when we came back as well. I loved the trips to the seaside. There used to be loads of buses, all parked up at the Back Way waiting to take everyone, about seven o'clock in the morning.

Sue Owen

We went to Rhyl with the Miners' Welfare

We went to Rhyl with the Miners' Welfare when we were little. We got on the train at Atherstone Station. We all had to queue up to get on and they gave us 10s, a bottle of pop and a packet of crisps. We thought it was great. We always went to the seaside with the Miners' Welfare. Every year Birch Coppice

The Coach and Horses Inn, Long Street, 1960.

pit had a gala day, it was lovely, they gave us a packed lunch and there was a fair, we thought it was wonderful.

Milly Thumbwood

We played in the cellars of the pub

After school we would go in the Coach & Horses pub. It was empty and going to be pulled down. There was me, Geoff and Steve Haddon and Martin Sweet, we played in the cellars of the pub and had a great time. There was loads and loads of bottles down in the cellars. We just used to look at everything down there. At the back of the Coach & Horses yard, we went into the old corn place as well. It used to be where the Council offices are now in South Street. The old Guide Hut was by the corn house. There were loads of places being knocked down at that time.

I was only a young lad, about twelve years old. It would be about 1972, I was at the High School. The High School had just gone Comprehensive with the Grammar School. We had some lessons at the Grammar School and others at the High School. We had to walk across from one school to the other.

I went and had a look around Vicki's Taxis place when that was empty. I found an old sales book, it was all handwritten in ink. It had all the sales in it from the Cattle Market. Vicki's Taxis place was next to where they used to have the Cattle Market. I was walking through the jitty by the swimming baths and a Copper stopped me and took it off me. I always wondered what happened to that book.

John Spragg

Dad took me to the jamborees

My dad, Harry Garratt, always took me to the Scout Jamborees, he was a Scoutmaster. I was born in 1936 so it would be the 1940s. My brother, Gordon Garratt, has a lot to do with the Scouts. We used to go to Atherstone Hall and the Scouts would practise up there, rifle shooting and swinging from one tree to the other. The Scouts used to be at the Salvation Army hut then in Grove Road.

Rita Deeming

I wanna be like you-ou-ou, Akala!

I joined the Atherstone Cubs in 1968. The Scout Hut is in Long Street next to the Dolphin pub. It was built where the old

Cotton Mill Yard used to be. The Guide Hut is the other side of the Dolphin pub, next to the Friendly Plaice chip shop. The 'Duck Pond' used to be there, can you remember? It was the old swimming baths, but we called it the 'Duck Pond' because it was so small. The Cub and Scout leaders were named after the *Jungle Book* characters, such as Akala and Kaa. The leaders were David and Edgar Penton. I remember doing 'Bob A Job' week all over the estate. I did all the jobs I hated doing, such as cleaning windows and cars. We had to do any job we were asked to do. When the money went decimal people paid 20p or 30p then. At the end of the week it would be announced who had collected the most money.

The Gang Shows were always a sell-out. They took place every two years, with other

The Atherstone Scout Band, 1911.

The Atherstone Scout Band 1972. Leading the band is Drum Major Peter Boyce and Paul Smith. Snare drummers, from left to right, are Tim Bonner, David Skeltcher, Andrew Rushton and Kevin Randall.

Troops and Guides in the district – Mancetter, Warton, Dordon and Grendon Sea Scouts. A Director would produce the Gang Show. Everyone else pitched in to make it all happen. I always remember Lenny Jacobs and Ernie Overton, they were always up for it, put their heart and soul into the Gang Show, making sure it was going to be great.

I moved up to the Scouts in 1971. We went camping in Luxembourg and Holland, they were the abroad camps. We took the band to Luxembourg on one of the camps. The Scout Band competed all over the country in competitions over here. The Scout leaders were Gordon Garratt, Mick Webber and Ernie Overton, Ernie Wykes was in charge of the band in the '70s. The 1st Atherstone Scout Band recorded an album called 'Tequila', I was the Mace Thrower in the band so I would

'chuck the stick up' as we say around here. I didn't play an instrument, so a picture of me was put on the outside back cover. I used to get some stick off my mates about being in Pickering's shop window, on the album cover. The album was so popular that the very last one was auctioned off. A while later a box full of the albums was found and mysteriously disposed of. When we competed in the Scouts National, I was Drum Major and I won 'Top Youth Drum Major Award' with 99½ points out of a possible 100. In the '70s, the 1st Atherstone Scouts Marching Band was doing extremely well. They banded well all over the country, including Basildon and Hornchurch, and competed in the main competition, the Scouts National. Mick Webber, one of our leaders, happened to be a barber in the town. It was the '70s remember, so long hair was fashionable. On Friday nights, if it was the night before a competition, Mick would cut our hair. There was no excuse, you couldn't say the barbers were shut. Into the '80s, the band was taken over by David Meads and Peter Boyce they were joint Band Masters. Eventually David Meads became in full charge when Peter Boyce left. The Band Instructors with him were Kevin Randall, Jimmy Duignan and myself, I had finished Drum Majoring. Within three years the band had reached its peak, winning the Scout Nationals for the first time ever. We came in the top five twice at Wembley, against every other top youth band in the country. Drum Major Nick Perry won several top titles at Wembley.

A very proud moment for all of us was when Princess Diana and Prince Charles came to Atherstone in 1985. They spoke to us all when we had finished the parade. Nick Perry and myself were invited to Windsor Castle as guests for a day. We met the Queen and our Mams and Dads travelled with us to Windsor Castle. We went into the Quadrangle at Windsor. The Scout Band were invited to the Royal Tournament in London, they

The Atherstone Cub Scouts football team, 1972.

The Atherstone Scouts football team, *c.* 1911.

put us in to do a spot. As far as the band went, I finished in 1986. I will never forget that in all those years, with the competitions we took part in all over the country where there were thousands of spectators, my most nerve-wracking experience was whenever we performed on the field at Atherstone Carnival. I used to look across and see all the familiar faces and go to pieces inside.

Paul Smith

four

Business and
Industry

The crater in the middle of town

I can remember an enormous crater on a piece of land in Long Street. It was where Foster's gentswear shop and Hilton's shoe shop was, opposite the old Co-op. There used to be a garage there where cars were repaired and it caught fire. The crater was there for years before they built the shops on the site.

George Morris

Long Street, 1950s.

Atherstone Fire Brigade, *c.* 1874. On the far right is leading fireman Joseph Deeming.

Bitsy the fire engine

Have you ever heard about Bitsy? Bitsy was a fire engine up at the Town Hall. It was made up of bits that were scrounged off different people in the town. My uncle Percy, Percy Bircher, told me about Bitsy years ago. There's the other fire engine as well, the horse-drawn one. When there was a fire my uncle Percy used to have to run to the field behind the back of the Angel and catch the horse first before the firemen could even go to the fire.

Gerry Barnes

I joined the fire brigade in 1939

On 3 September 1939 I joined the Atherstone Fire Brigade. It was the start of the Second World War. The Fire Brigade was called out many times during the war, to Ansley, Nuneaton, Coventry and Birmingham. The fire station used to be where Wainwright's garage now stands. It has also been underneath the Town Hall that used to be in the Market Square. They built a new fire station down Ratcliffe Road in the 1950s. I retired from the Fire Service in 1965 to work as the manager at Megginson's ironmongers in Church Street. I retired in 1976.

Sidney Pratt

Shops galore – 1930s

I was born in Richmond Road and moved to Lagoes Buildings when I was a youngster. There was no need to go to any other town, Atherstone sold everything. There were tobacconists, sweet shops, newsagents, printers, toy shops, record shops, book shops,

The Atherstone police station and Magistrate's Court, Ratcliffe Road (Dog Lane), 1960s. Warwick House and Cooke's Chemist are now situated on the site.

paint and wallpaper shops, greengrocers, shoe shops, herbalists, chemists, bike shops, clothes shops, hardware shops, bakers and butchers. Johnny Schofield owned an off-licence and was a professional goalkeeper for Birmingham City in his day. Tunbridge's, Fox's and Frost's butchers each had their own slaughterhouse at the rear of their shops where they killed the animals to sell for food. Vic Starr was an auctioneer who traded in Fords yard. Frank Clarke's shop later became 'Pipers Bazaar', a shop very similar to Woolworth's, it had swinging doors like the saloon doors you see in cowboy films. Hiscock's department store sold furniture, carpets, household goods, clothes and lingerie. It was a massive shop just on the corner of Market Street. Jack Hapely traded as the rag and bone man in Meads yard.

Jack was a very smart man who traded in salt too, in Lagoes buildings. The salt was stored in solid blocks about 2ft by 9in in size. Freeman's pop factory was situated in the Black Boy yard. Vanta pop was sold on premises behind Tunbridge's, and was owned by the Guild family. Dickie Askew made and sold delicious pork batches and Sam Deeming's fish and chip shop was very popular. Even the nuns at the convent cashed in with their home produce. There was a small hatch door through which you would hear the voice of a nun ask what it was you wanted. A basket would appear with apples or eggs etc. We had to pay by putting the money into the empty basket and placing it back onto the hatch.

George Morris

The butcher liked a drink or two

Johnson's Charabancs used to be next to the George & Dragon pub in Long Street years ago. There was a bakery in Coleshill Road, next to the Billiard Hall. If anyone had a big bird for the oven, they would cook it in their large ovens for a small fee. Mrs Haddon who lived in Allens Row, used to work for the council collecting the bodies of people who had died. She pushed a big trolley that had big wheels and handles on it. She could only just get up some entries because they were narrow. Once she had put the body on the trolley, she would take them to the mortuary and lay them out. The butchers used to go to the Cattle Market in Station Street and buy the livestock such as bulls and cows. The Blacksmiths was in Station Street behind the Square & Compass pub. They could get the horses shod while they went to the sale. The Three Tuns, Red Lion and the Blue Bell all had stables at the back. The local butchers in the town would buy livestock from the Cattle Market and slaughter them in the back of the yards where their slaughterhouses were. There was one butcher who liked a drink or two, if you know what I mean! Most of the men drank in those days, it was cheap enough, they only had mild and bitter in the pubs. Anyway, he used to tell us to 'clear off' when we were watching him, there used to be a crowd of us. There weren't any tellies in them days, so this is what we did, watch the blacksmiths or the butchers. Anyway, we still used to stand and watch him and took no notice of him. He used a poleaxe to slaughter the animals, I don't know if you have ever noticed the metal rings around the town, up where the yards used to be? The butchers used to pull the rope through the ring to hold the beast still so that it couldn't move. My dad told me that one day when he was a young lad he and his mates watched the butcher as he swung the poleaxe to kill a beast, he missed and instead he hit it

above the eye. The eye shot out of its socket, you can imagine how big it was. All these kids jumped back frit to death, they never moved so fast in their lives.

Derek Smith

Jane's curiosity shop

I purchased the shop in 2000 when Jane Stafford died and the shop was put up for sale. The parchment deeds to the shop date back to 1740, but it is possible the shop is actually older than that. The document mentions 'The sharing of the well and pump', the 'murk and rubbish' and lots of information about 'rights of passage' of the other inhabitants in dwellings close by. William Freer, tanner, is mentioned in the conveyances. It is really interesting when you read it. Apparently, so I'm told, some of the aristocracy came to the shop when Jane Stafford owned it. Some people would be on their way to the shipping ports and stop off in Atherstone to buy their ball gowns, ready for the cruises they were going on. It wasn't unusual to see a Rolls Royce parked outside in the '40s and '50s. Jane Stafford had purchased the shop in 1946 and had left behind a wonderful collection of clothes and millinery. The items dated back to the 1930s. It was just like Christmas, I was like an excited child, never knowing what I was going to find next as I looked through drawers, cupboards and wardrobes. There were dolls and toys in the attic, wrapped in their original packaging with the old price tags on them in pounds, shillings and dimes.

Janice Breedan

Jane Stafford's

Jane Stafford was a respected, likeable and well-known lady who would never let you leave her shop looking anyhow. She would help dress you and make suggestions about

A group of local models at a Jane Stafford Mannequin Parade, 1950s. Jane Stafford is on the far left of the photograph.

what would suit you. Nothing was too much trouble for Jane. Years ago I couldn't afford to buy my clothes there, but when I got older and got married I did. You had to be pretty well-off to buy from her shop. Years ago all the posh people went there.

Gladys Jewell

Fittings by appointment
Jane Stafford used to organise Mannequin Parades at the Parish Rooms, the Guide Hut and the Senior School. She raised funds for lots of local charities. I used to go to her shop for my lingerie wear; you had to make an appointment to have a fitting. She would measure you up in the room at the back of the shop to make sure that the fit was perfect.

Phyllis Morris

Cosy Toes café
We had the Cosy Toes café in Long Street when I came out of the Army and Tom Ryder came out of the Air Force. It was after the war had finished. Me, Beryl and Tom and Dorothy Ryder owned it between us. It used to be Dickie Askew's place. Mrs Gisbourne

Above: The Cosy Toes café, second building on the left, in the 1950s.

Right: The damaged Cosy Toes café shop front, after the car accident, 1950s. Jean Chetwynd, who worked at the café, surveys the damage.

Thomas Beck's saddlers at No. 125 Long Street, *c.* 1910. The young man is Charles Beck, the son of the said Thomas Beck. The shop was later known as Kingshorne's, Cooke and Ryder's, and is currently Billy's Moonshine.

had the tobacconist next door, she supplied everyone in the town with tobacco. One day, it was around 1950, she was in her car and accelerated backwards, straight into the shop front. It smashed all the front of the shop in. We moved to the Hall Lane in Coleshill Road and then up to Long Street next to where the Somerfield supermarket is. We sold everything in the shop – Dinky toys and Corgie toys and lots of other toys and sports equipment. If we hadn't got it in stock we would get it. It was a fairyland shop to come into.

Charles Cooke

I was a grocer boy in the 1920s

My grandad was James Beale, he was the licensee for forty-eight years at the White Lion, known to locals as Sweeties. He had a family of thirteen children. Uncle Bert Beale had the grocer shop next door. I was about ten years old when I'd call everyday after school to help out at the shop. When I was twelve years old in 1921 I had a grocery round. I used a sack truck on wheels to deliver the groceries. It would be filled with bags of grocery orders ready for me to take to the houses. Some of the women would call in the shop on their way to work at the factories, to order the food. I walked all around town, up and down

Simmond's Bros, fruit & potato merchants, *c.* 1920.

the yards, doing my deliveries. Some families would have the orders on the 'slate' whereby they would come into the shop and pay the bill on Fridays (pay day). Others would leave the money on the table. No one locked their doors, there was no need to – you would rather give to your neighbours than take from them. Everyone helped each other out in those days.

Sidney Pratt

Home-grown produce

I can remember Patsy Reid. He lived in the Cotton Mill yard. Patsy used to have an allotment in North Street where he grew his own fruit and vegetables. He would go all around the town selling his stuff, on his horse and dray.

Charlie Ross

Packed full of shoppers

When I left school I used to work in a shop called the Star. Later it changed to George Mason's grocery store. It used to be where the craft shop is now. Savers used to be the Maypole. On Saturday afternoons in the '50s and '60s the town was packed full with shoppers. We used to get lots of people coming through the town.

Nancy Lees

A grocer boy in the '60s

I worked at Melias' shop; it used to be where the Nationwide Building Society is now. They gave me a big black bike that had a basket on the front to put the groceries in. I used to deliver groceries to houses up Merevale Lane and Mancetter. If I had to deliver up to Baddesley, I caught the Evans's bus.

John Freeman

The tannery was here

There's a stone plaque in the brickwork behind my shop. It is inscribed W.F. 1803. There used to be a tannery behind here, it belonged to William Freer. My shop at No. 10 Church Street used to be Joseph Woods' shop, where leather boots and shoes were made.

Gerry Barnes

The mail man came from Luton

My dad's grandad, Joseph Deeming, used to drive the coach and horses up to the Red Lion Hotel from Luton. He was born in Luton in 1796. He brought the mail and parcels to Atherstone. There were stables behind the Red Lion where they stabled the horses overnight. Joseph used to come to Atherstone every week, he met a local girl and they were

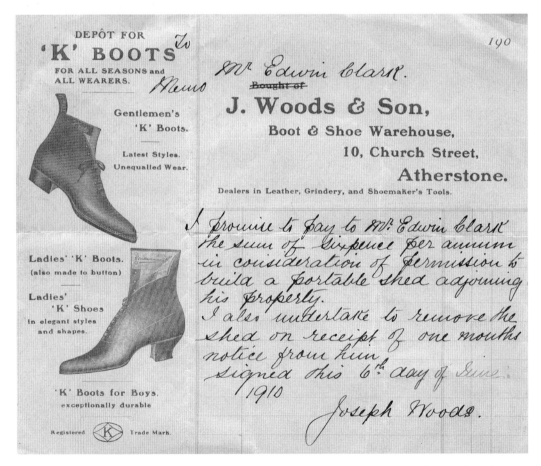

A memo from Joseph Woods, promising to pay Mr Edwin Clark 'sixpence per annum in consideration of permission to build a portable shed adjoining his property', in 1910.

Polly Windridge and Emily Dingley with two young children in the pushchair, Long Street, c. 1930.

married. Their son, Joseph Deeming, was the leading fireman in the Atherstone Fire Brigade around 1874. He knew where every single water pump was in the town. My dad was Sam Deeming. He was the night operator in the '30s at the old post office, and worked 8 a.m. to 8 p.m. and at weekends for 11s a week. The rent and lighting was free, this was before telephones went automatic. He and my mum Lottie had the fish and chip shop opposite the Old Swan for twenty-nine years before they sold it in the 1960s.

Eveline Johnson

We lived on the barges

I came to live in Atherstone when my mum and dad decided to stay here, after stopping off on the Coventry canal at Atherstone. We lived on the barges for years and came up from Oxford originally. There were plenty of factories in the town and it was easy to get a job. I married Sid and had three children: Beryl, David and Tony. I started work at Vero's laundry, where my wages were £2 a week. I worked with Winnie Fretwell, Winnie Blower and Doll Barlow. Emily Dingley worked there as well. Downstairs in the workshop there were two big boilers. The wet washing would

The demolition of Vero's laundry in the 1960s.

be put into a truck and pushed across the yard to another workshop. Beat Chapman and me worked together, we'd put the sheets through a big roller to press all the water out. I would put it through one end and Beat would pull the sheets through the other end. Then we would fold all the dry washing ready for the packing room. Women who ironed the shirts were called press-hands. Two men would collect the washing in a van. They went to the hospital twice a week as well as collecting it from the big houses. Mrs Vero's Laundry Shop was in Long Street. The men called there to collect washing, because a lot of customers took their washing to the Laundry Shop. I didn't have far to go to work, we lived in the yard next door, the Post Sorting Office is there now. You can still see part of the old laundry wall, on the left-hand side of the Safeway car park.

Dorothy Cheshire

Woodcocks Iron Foundry

When I left school I was fourteen years old and I went to work at Woodcocks Iron Foundry in North Street, I used to get ten bob a week, that's 50p nowadays. It was in 1934, we melted the scrap metal and made manhole covers and drain covers and things like that. Places like Megginson's would buy them to sell to the builders. The moulds were in sand and we had to ram them with the sand. One day I was outside, pouring the hot liquid metal in the moulder. It was damp in the sump and it all blew back at me, I was badly burnt. Jacky Gamber and Fred Yeatman and some others took their caps off and kept patting the flames on me, trying to put them out, I was on fire. I spent three weeks in the Manor hospital. When I joined the Navy later on and had my examination, I was covered in scars.

Charlie Ross

They have all vanished

The steam trains with coal fires glowing in the dark, the lamplighter lighting the gas lamps and the knife-grinder have all vanished. The memory of them though is still vivid.

Sylvia Rose Burgess

Mr Hatton was a true gentleman

After the war I went back to Denham's hat factory for a bit. I did 'sizing', I had to stick labels inside the hats, of the size that they were. There were lots of different sizes and styles of hats, there were Trilbys, Ghurkha hats, Egyptian Fezs and a whole lot more. We sent them all over the world. In the 1950s I went to work at Hatton's hat factory, in the Hardening Shop. That was hard work that was, I tell you it was. The wool for the hats came from the formers upstairs. I had to press it onto a big press and turn it over and press the other side. The presses were hot and very heavy to pull down. I did this all day long. We had to smooth them with our hands once they had been pressed and stack them into piles ready to go to the next department. The factory was big really, but small compared to the other hat factories in the town. Mr Hatton was a true gentleman, very approachable and thought a lot of his workers. We had a Christmas party every year, in the Trimming Room, Mr Hatton supplied everything.

Beryl Gilliver

The factory girls walked arm in arm

I used to love to see the young girls from the factories walk arm in arm down to Winnie's café, in the Backway. I used to see them laughing and joking and looking so happy.

The Bulls Head pub, *c.* 1910.

A worker outside Hatton's Hat Factory, carrying out one of the many processes of felt hat making. Notice the felt hoods on the ground.

Sometimes they would be singing and then stop to light up their cigarettes. I worked on inspection at the knitwear factory in the 1960s. I can still see them now in my mind. I thought they were nice girls, they were very down to earth and always spoke to you. It's a shame the kids don't seem to enjoy themselves so much these days do they?

Elsie Swann

The bumping shop

There were a lot of us who worked in the bumping shop at Vero & Everitt's hat factory. Some of the people had worked there all their lives. Alf Pare, a foreman, and Tom King had worked there since they left school I believe. I started there in the late '70s, I'd never worked in a factory before. The bumping shop was quite a big place. At the far end was the door which led into the knitwear factory. The bumpers bumped mechanically all day long, big metal arms that went up and down pounding the felt. Then there were rollers, where we would turn the felt hoods inside out and put them through about four or five times, turning them each time. One of us would stand at one end to put the hoods through and someone would stand at the other end. Backwards and forwards they went until they

Megginson's yard, 2001. This yard was a popular passageway, leading from the lower end of town into Church Street. On the far left is Hatton's hat factory (now dilapidated).

were ready to be stacked and put into trucks, ready for the next process. The bumping shop was wet and steamy, we wore Wellingtons and plastic aprons. There wasn't a canteen, we had our food and drink at a wooden table, the same place where we worked, at break time. We had some good times at the factory, everyone worked together and got on well with each other. Over the road was the millinery, where the women trimmed the hats. There were all kind of hats made for this country and abroad.

Beryl Freeman

Khaki hats

I worked in the Packing Department for Michael Stafford at Wilson & Staffords, when I left school. It was my very first job in 1976. The thing I always remember about that first job was all the khaki hats that were sent to Nigeria for their Armed Forces. The hats used to be packed into big wooden crates.

John Spragg

Trimming hats by candlelight

When I was a young girl, I used to fetch my mother's hats from Wilson & Stafford's hat factory in my dinner hour. My mother made a

A canal-side view of Wilson & Staffords hat factory, Coleshill Road.

Wilson & Staffords box factory workers in the 1930s. Back row: Nora Kenyan, Gertie Ben, Marion Deville. Front row: Mary Ford, Florence Killian.

big black sack to put the hats in. I had to carry the bag all the way up the stairs to a trap door. Sometimes the bag was so heavy that I had to drag it up the stairs. The Foremistress would take it off me and then give me another bagful to take home. I did this every day before I ate my lunch and went back to school. At night, me and my mother sat by the window in the living room trimming hats. It was lighter by the window, we could see the thread better for threading the needles. We sometimes worked in the candlelight, sewing bands, bows and ribbons onto the hats. When I was fourteen years old I worked at Wilson & Staffords as a 'Day Girl'. I used to have to carry the work from one department to another. After a year I was trained to sew the leather bands on inside

the hats by hand. A few years afterwards, they brought sewing machines in and now we were able to machine the bands onto the hats.

Ellen Mills

Pen pal

I worked at Hatton's hat factory when I left school. I worked in the trimming department, as a machinist. We sewed ribbons and bands on the hats. There were all types of hats, lots of different styles, they went all over the world. Some of the girls used to write their names and addresses on pieces of paper and put them inside the boxes of hats. They hoped that someone would write back and be a pen pal.

Gladys Allcock

Mrs Knight, Gladys Allcock and Polly Richardson leaving work at Hatton's hat factory, 1935.

It was easier to kick the bag

When my mum left the factory to have us, it was my turn to fetch the hats. Mum trimmed the hats at home like many other mums did. It was easier to kick the bag all the way down the road, because it was so heavy. It scrunched up at the top and was as big as I was.

Jean Mills

Joseph Lester Vero

Joseph Lester Vero was the founder of the J.L. Vero slipper factory. The Vero family had a business in Atherstone since the middle of the nineteenth century. From 1870 the factory – Britannia Works – was engaged in the manufacture of socks and footwear sundries. It was generally known as the 'sock factory' up until the Second World War. It expanded rapidly from the late '20s when new buildings were erected to accommodate the manufacture of sheepskin slippers and webbing sandals. Production was curtailed during the war, when a modern block was taken over as an Engineering Works for the war effort. Post-war production expanded again and eventually shoemaking machinery was installed. At its peak the company employed a hundred people. Following difficult trading conditions the family sold the business in 1989. Production ceased within two years.

Clifford Vero

J.L. Vero slipper factory

I started at J.L. Vero in 1963. J.L. Vero was a well-known slipper and sandal firm. It was a very old building, but very effective. The

Bertram Vero and Clifford Vero amongst the well-wishers at the J.L. Vero slipper factory, on the retirement of Major Vero (far right).

firm dealt with real hides and sheepskins. The Vero family ran the firm, Major Vero, Clifford and Roy Vero. It was very much a family business. When we started to make the slippers and sandals, it was like one big jigsaw puzzle. We would start down in the 'clicking' room where every little part was cut to make up the slippers and sandals. After we in the 'clicking' room had finished cutting, they were stuck together, before going upstairs on the elevator. The work would be examined before coming back down to the 'clicking' room. There would be a box with the uppers inside, a box with linings and another box with soles inside. Once the work had gone back upstairs after being examined again it would start on its rounds – gluing, stitching, and stitching the name tabs on the soles. You can imagine what high-class footwear they were, when I tell you the names of Russell & Bromley, Dolcis, Marks & Spencer, Vitchell & Bromley, Lilley & Skinner, all of those were very good customers of ours. There were others, but I can't remember all of their names now. The work was examined after each process. It had to be perfect. We had some very fine machinists, they knew exactly how to do a perfect job. So the puzzle was taking shape. The next stage was, that the slippers and sandals went to another room where the men worked on the heavy machinery. This was where the men worked on the 'lasts'. While all these various jobs were being done, you could hear the shop floor chit-chat, singing and joking of the workers, over the noises from the machines. It was a very happy place to work. Ron Windridge who worked on the 'lasts' would examine everything again. Finally, the finished products were packed. The bosses would be in the factory, walking up and down, making sure the work was right. I can still see Mr Clifford peering down his nose, looking to see if we were doing the work right. I can remember a very big special order, which was being sent to Canada. Our slippers and sandals weren't just made for the British market, they were sent all over the world. I can still remember the great sense of pride we all felt, when this big order was finished, boxed and sent to Canada. They weren't just ordinary slippers and sandals that were made at J.L. Vero. They were beautiful slippers and sandals.

Gwen Johnson

When I was a lad – 1930s

There wasn't a lot of money around in those days, nearly everyone would wear hand-me-downs. It was normal to wear trousers with patches sewn onto them, most people had large families and you were grateful for what you had. I left school in 1931, it was either mining or working in the hat factories, you were sure to get a job. I chose mining because the pay was higher. A weeks wage was 17s 6d, with an increase of 6d a week after six months, making a week's pay 18s. Mining and hatting was thirsty work, it's no wonder there were so many pubs in Atherstone. We looked forward to our weekends. The manager was Mr Wardle, a true gentleman, who had a great deal of respect for the workmen. The siren would sound five minutes before the shift began. This would give everyone time to collect their safety lamps from the lamp cabin. Each lamp was numbered so that if the shift ended and a lamp was missing it meant that the miner would still be down the mine. Before going down, we were searched. If a nubbed cigarette or match was found on anyone, they would be liable to a 10s fine and sometimes sent home. Going down in the cage was the scariest experience. The cage would thud when you got to the bottom of the shaft. I did get used to it after a week or so. We hung our snap onto hooks down the pit, where there were millions of mice. If you just happened to forget, there

Sir William Stratford Dugdale – Lord of the Manor. He lost his life after the failed rescue attempts to save eight men and a boy entombed in the Baddesley Mine explosion of 1882.

Baddesley Colliery, with the pit shaft in the background, in the 1930s. Sir William Dugdale is with his nine-year-old son, who later became Sir William Dugdale.

would be holes in the snap, where the mice had nibbled their way through it.

There was a lot of water at the bottom of Baddesley pit, it would find its way to the pump house at Speedwell Lane, known locally as Watery Lane, in Baddesley village. The water would be pumped into the shaft, then flow through the tunnel, which went down underneath the Watling Street and into the River Anker. The local children would learn to swim in the shaft. But there were some terrible accidents; children were ripped on the barbed wire that surrounded the shaft. The water level would sometimes rise above the barbed wire, and the children couldn't see it. Many a man lost a limb or an eye in the pit, leaving them disabled. The cable wire caused lots of accidents. During my time as a miner I'd seen men lose legs and arms due to the cable being wrapped around them.

I can remember Pooley Hall and Kingsbury mines would have pit ponies. They used to bring the ponies up and put bags over their eyes, preventing them being exposed to daylight, as they had worked in the dark the whole time. We had some good times as well you know; we used to have a laugh. One thing I remember was when we were walking towards the baths with just our towels wrapped around us, one of my mates didn't bother wrapping a towel around him. The nurse was a rather large, robust lady. She was standing by the baths and my mate was so embarrassed at seeing her that he ran off. The nurse shouted, 'Don't worry, I've seen bigger things at the school.' We were all in fits of laughter. At the candy wharf, behind the blue brick cottage there would be three or four men shovelling coal onto the barges from the coal wagons. The barges turned around at the wharf, where there's a basin. The family who loaded the barges were the Chapman family who lived in Baddesley in the 1930s. The blue brick cottage stands on the Watling Street

by Holly Lane Island, a level crossing was positioned from one side of the Watling Street to the other. The Atherstone miners would get on board the pit train, which travelled up along the Paddy Line up to Baddesley Colliery.

I retired from the pit when I was sixty-eight years old. My dad worked down the pit when he was eleven years old and worked there all his life. He told me that when the men walked up Merevale Lane from Atherstone on 1 May 1882, the sky was lit up by the Aurora Borealis (the Northern Lights), a luminous electromagnetic phenomenon seen in the sky. My dad told me that the Atherstone miners took this to be an omen and returned home. That was the night the mine exploded and eight men and a boy were entombed down the mine. Others got killed trying to rescue them, including Sir William Stratford Dugdale. The Dugdales owned the pit then, before the National Coal Board took it over.

George Knight

Grandad was entombed

My dad was George Atkins, he worked at Baddesley pit. His dad was a miner, and was one of those who were entombed in the May mine disaster.

Margaret Owen

At the pit

William Blower, who was killed in the Baddesley mine disaster, was my grandad. When I was fourteen years old I worked underground at the pit, my twin brother Fred worked there as well. I was very concerned about Fred's safety, I worried about him all the time, he was smaller than me. The cage went down to the pit bottom so quickly it was frightening, it would thud as it touched the ground. Chris Grubb who lived next

Coal miners at Baddesley Colliery, *c*. 1950.

door to the Maid of the Mill used to lend me his bike for 6d. I could ride to work then from Coleshill Road. Most of the Atherstone miners would get to the pit along the Paddy Line. My job was 'clipping', but when we were working, water would be dripping through the seams of the roof and we'd have to keep filling up the bottles with it.

Sidney Pratt

Safety was paramount at Baddesley pit

I started work at the pit in 1980. My first job was Banksman up at the 'Old Pit' top.

There were three of us who were Banksmen, one for each shift – days, afternoons and nights. The three of us worked rotating shifts. Malc Downs trained me for my job for about a month. My job as a Banksman was to put the men on the cage and signal to the winder in the Winding House. This was to let him

know it was clear to wind the men down the shaft in the cage. There were so many safety checks to do before the men actually went down in the cage in the mineshaft. Someone at the bottom of the pit would buzz to say it was all clear. I pressed the buzzer to say it was all clear at the top. I would press three times to say my men were riding. Once everyone had signalled each other the all clear, the winder would automatically start to descend. Safety was paramount, all safety devices were checked every day. All the miners had a set of tallies, one bronze and one silver. The tallies had a number on to identify each miner. The miners would hand me the silver tally and I would send them in a canister up the Air-Shoot, up to the Time Office. The miners carried the brass ones with them. When they came back up the shaft on the cage, they had to hand their brass tallies to me. I would then send them to the Time Office to show that

John Spragg standing in the head gear of the winders at the old pit.

Among the people in the 'new' Winding House are Brian Haddon, Abba ?, David Spragg and Joe Chetwynd, 1980s.

they were back up safe from down the pit. All the controls at the pit were changed to electronic. Sometimes if it broke down we worked the system manually. We had Benny Catchers at the pit – another safety device. If anything went wrong with the winding gear the cages would go up to the Benny Catchers at the very top and then automatically knock the system out.

It was always my ambition to go down to the 'Old Workings' at Baddesley. One Friday night, Walter Chambers, one of the Senior Overmen at the pit took me down. There was always a Senior Manager at the pit. There would be a Deputy, an Overman, and a Senior Overman. The old mine carts were still down there, railway lines and all the old workings It was really interesting to see the difference of how mining was then, in the old days. A stone plaque was down there, with the inscription on to 'Sir William Dugdale, 1882'. Behind the plaque was where the entombed miners perished, eight men and a young boy, it was eerie. Baddesley and Baxterley had half of a wheel each placed in the villages, taken from the 'Old Windings' to commemorate these two mining villages. Baddesley Colliery was situated in the villages of Baxterley and Baddesley, which were next to each other. In 1989 the Baddesley pit closed, we couldn't quite believe it could happen, but it did.

John Spragg

five

Social and Leisure

My dad was in the Atherstone Orchestra

My dad was in the Atherstone Orchestra, they played at the Corn Exchange where the old Picture House used to be. The orchestra played at the Coffee Tavern, before my time. My dad told me all about it. They used to call the orchestra Pickerings Band. My dad played the violin, Fred Lunn played the drums and Bert Richardson played the piano and the three of them used to play at the Co-op Hall and the Parish Rooms. I don't know if they called themselves anything in particular, they used to play most Saturday nights. There used to be a roller-skating rink in Atherstone you know, I think it was in Station Street. You're talking about the '30s or '40s.

Charlie Ross

The way we was initiated

I was christened by Canon Northcote at St Mary's church and Dr Praisey was my godfather. It was customary to go to church every Sunday; it was the way you were brought up. Nearly everyone went to church. I joined the boys' choir when I was old enough. Opposite the church in the Market Place was a big water trough for the horses. Once you joined the boys' choir you were dipped in the trough, this was the way you were initiated. Canon George Mathews from Sheepy took us all on holiday to Wales for two weeks. We went to Brinkadefore, near Barmouth. His father was a priest in the village, he let us stay

in the School House. George Evans drove us down on an Evans bus and stayed for the whole two weeks taking us out. Atherstone was a great little town, everyone was 'uncle' to me. I knew all of the landlords at the pubs and the people who lived in the yards. These days at the age of eighty-six I rarely venture out.

Wilf Deeming

Merevale Park flower show

The annual flower show was held on August Bank Holiday Monday in Merevale Park. After races, the judging of the exhibits and having tea in the stuffy tents, the show ended with a firework display. The rockets soared up into the sky and as they descended in a shower of coloured lights, they were greeted with long drawn out 'oohs' and 'aahs' from the appreciative children.

Sylvia Rose Burgess

The Statutes fair

In September there was the Statutes – a yearly fair which took place on the third weekend of the month. Originally farm workers, milkmaids and domestic workers were hired out for the year. The milkmaids carried a pail and farm workers wore straw in their caps to signify their occupation. The stalls of gingerbread etc. used to stretch right down Coleshill Road to the Red Lion. The

The Atherstone Orchestra, at the rear of Pickering's shop, 1900. Charlie Ross's father, Walter, is seen sitting second from left in the front row at the age of fourteen.

swings and roundabouts were erected in the Market Place, which was then in South Street. It was mostly children who went to the fair on Saturday afternoon, but adults patronised it in the evening, especially on Tuesday. The cost of a ride then rose from one penny, and twopence, to threepence and the rides became shorter and shorter as the evening wore on. There would be several customers waiting to scramble into the cars, or onto the horses the moment the music stopped. It was a great thrill when one of my brothers would tell me to sit tight and stay on for another round.

Sylvia Rose Burgess

The Statutes fair in the '30s and '40s

The Statutes was up Long Street, the Back Way and the Hall Lane by the Bulls Head pub. There was the Helter Skelter, the Cake-Walk and the Carousel. Side stalls such as Roll-a-Penny, Coconut Shies, the Penny Arcades and the Wall of Death (motorbikes). There were midgets or very fat people who performed in the Freak Show. The boxing ring used to be pitched up in the Back Way for anyone who wanted to fight for prize money. There were peacocks lit up all around the place and dragons and crocodiles. The shops stayed open until late at night. The town had gas street lamps in those days, so we would watch the lamplighter as well.

Phyllis Morris

White channels down their black faces

After Christmas was over the next excitement was Shrove Tuesday, when the shops would be boarded up and the townsfolk would kick a large, oval-shaped ball up and down Long Street. There were no pit baths then so miners with black coaldust still on their faces would join in the game straight from their shift. The sweat made white channels down their black faces as the crowd heaved and jostled each other to get possession of the ball. I watched the progress of the game excitedly from an upstairs window.

Sylvia Rose Burgess

We all ended up in the canal

When I was only a young girl I went to the Ball Game on Shrove Tuesday every year, everyone did. There were no rules to the game then about how far it could go. It went anywhere and everywhere in the town. Up and down the yards, up the back alleys, in people's sheds, and even in people's houses years ago. You just went with the crowd.

Anyway this one year we were dragged along with everyone else and we all ended up in the canal. There were loads of people in there, we were all wet through.

Milly Evans

Barclays came to the rescue

For years the ball had been thrown from the balcony of the Blue Bell, Three Tuns and then Cooke and Ryders shop. We thought the Ball Game would have to come to an end when Cooke and Ryders closed down. We spoke to the manager of Barclays Bank and luckily he and the powers that be helped us out. Every year it was customary to invite a well-known celebrity to throw out the ball. Years ago it was always the principal actor starring in the

Wilf Deeming's uncle Piddy was the ball winner in 1910. The picture was taken outside the Hat & Beaver pub.

Sir William Dugdale, holding the ball, is standing on the window ledge of the Blue Bell Inn, in the 1920s.

Christmas pantomime at the Coventry Theatre who would be invited, or a well-known sports celebrity. George Formby, Beryl Reid, Ken Dodd, Jimmy Tarbuck, Larry Grayson, Brian Little and Gordon Banks are just a few of the celebrities who have been over the years. We asked our own local sporting personality to throw the ball out, in more recent years – Paul Broadhurst, the golfer. The golden penny is thrown out first, the winner receives £10. Then when the ball is thrown out, whoever gets the ribbons wins £10 for each ribbon. There's a red, blue and white ribbon attached to the ball. There have been two occasions when a black ribbon was attached to the ball. Once when Bertie Ford died, he devoted much of his time to the Ball Game. Another time was when Joey Eiken died, he was known as one of the fiercest competitors of the time in the '40s. Sweets are donated from various businesses, which are thrown to the kids in the crowd by the boxful. We have a sponsor from a local business to fund the game each year, Brian Keates was this year's sponsor. Stuart Morcom and his brother, Adrian, come every year from Wales, both originally Atherstone lads. They take action photographs and give them to me to add to our collection. Rules had to be applied in the '70s and stewards were appointed for safety measures, Rocky King and Harold Taft sort that out. Phil Read donates the £30 ribbon-winner money. Paul Groucott and Mick DeSylva are on the committee as well. We have a good, strong, committee who are dedicated to the 800-year-old tradition. According to legend, it was in the reign of King John, crowned in 1199, that a football game was played between the Atherstone lads and the Leicestershire lads at Witherley, and has been played here ever since that time. The NWBC Mayor and Deputy Mayor with the Town Council Mayor are invited to come along each year. We all meet up at the Angel Inn in the Market Place,

After the Ball Game was over, it was customary to hold a ballroom dance in the evening. Mrs Lillie Propert (left) sits with two friends wearing their ballgowns, c. 1920.

Johnny Ball, Bert Powell Snr, Nobby, Bummy Chetwynd, Flo and Bert Powell (landlord and landlady), Mr Sanders (Mayor) with actress and comedienne Beryl Reid, at The Blue Bell Inn, c. 1953..

Bill Dixon, president of the Ball Game Committee, throws the ball out from the window of Barclays Bank.

where a buffet is put on, before going to Barclays Bank. The winner is the person who has got the ball at 5.00 p.m., Rocky King makes the final decision. The police, Rocky, and the stewards escort the winner back to the Angel Inn where we all celebrate afterwards. The winner always goes around the town for a few weeks with the ball and collects money for the charity of their choice. The winner is also allowed to keep the ball. The youngest recorded winner was seventeen-year-old Tom Jackson.

Bill Dixon

The travelling theatre

There used to be a travelling theatre called The Holloways in the 1930s. They came from Cannock and travelled all around, right to Leicester. They would come to Atherstone at the same time each year. They used to set up on land by the Kings Head. They had seats for everyone to sit on and the staging. Mr Holloway had two daughters – Leah and Mona. My dad's youngest brother, uncle Alf Bonner, used to rehearse with the theatre company and Mr Holloway said, 'Why don't you come with us?' He packed his job up and

Mona Holloway, an actress with the travelling theatre, is seen here in the 1930s.

Alfred Bonner, an actor with the travelling theatre, is seen here as Cecil Stroud in *Why Girls Go Wrong*, in the 1930s.

travelled with them. Uncle Alf and Mona got married eventually. I wish I could tell you more about my family, you know, but you just didn't ask questions years ago.

Celestine Bonner

Life is a stage

They used to come down through the town, under the Cattle Arch along the Old Watling Street and up to the field by the Kings Head. They used to do a show about Nurse Edith Cavell who served in the First World War. Kids used to go on Saturday afternoons. It cost a penny or a ha'penny for kids, Mrs Holloway would give them an orange to eat when they got to the tent. The factory workers used to collect money for the Holloways and give them the money. At night the factory girls would go and watch the show, they all went together in a gang. They were good actors and actresses you know, the Holloways were. When they were going to the tent the kids used to say, 'We are going to the Blood Tub tonight', they got the saying from somewhere. When Mrs Holloway died she was buried in Atherstone cemetery. There is a big stone angel with a verse inscribed which goes 'Life is a stage and although you've played your part/ Death cannot sever the love in our hearts'.

Dorothy Walton

There were very few cars

There were very few cars in the 1920s, consequently the streets were much quieter and safer to walk in when I was a young girl. Walking was quite a popular leisure activity then. We would go the children's swings near the railway line. Besides swinging, we would watch the mailbag being snatched from the train by a special wooden contraption.

Sylvia Rose Burgess

The charabanc

It wasn't luxury in the way of comfort, but oh we did enjoy ourselves. It used to be such a thrill to go for a ride in the charabanc. I remember when we were at Mancetter School, we went to Sutton Park for the day. Our headmistress warned us to sit still or we could distract the driver, and that we would be taken off if we didn't sit still. It was a bit bumpy, but we didn't care. Most of the time we had to walk when we went anywhere. We sang all the way there and all the way back, it was great. I was born in 1915, so it would have been about 1922.

Emily Dewis

The Salvation Army were our salvation

The Salvation Army always got a summer trip up to take everyone out for the day. They

Didn't they have a lovely time – families enjoying a day out in a charabanc, 1925.

paid for everything. We went to Sutton Park, Alton Towers and Trentham Gardens. They always gave a lovely Christmas party. The Salvation Army was very much aware that a lot of Atherstone kids were not well off. I can remember my mam telling me that during the big strike in the '30s, they gave the kids a breakfast every day.

Jean Neville

A pig's bladder for a football

It was called Frosts yard where we lived, after Freddie Frost the butcher from years ago, although the nameplate used to have Winters Terrace on it. If you can imagine, the butchers shop was at the front of the yard on Long Street. As you walked up the yard there were four houses, Mr Oxford (the butcher) and Mrs Oxford lived in one, then Mr and Mrs Chapman, Mr and Mrs Smalley and then us (Ellen and Bill were our mum and dad), then there was the place where the butcher made the sausages, then you came to the slaughterhouse. We used to watch him through the slats in the doors. Next to there was a stable where he kept the livestock. We would watch him drag the pig ready to shoot, but once he got the gun we made a run for it back down the yard. Bang! You could hear the gun fire then we would run back and ask if we could have the pig's bladder. We blew the bladder up to make a football while it was wet. My grandad led the Sunday treats procession, holding a pig's bladder up in the air on a big stick. My aunt Iris tells me that he used to tap the children on the head, for a bit of fun, while they were marching through the streets.

Jean Mills

Fined for playing football

My mum's brother, uncle Ernie, got fined once when they lived in the Nelson yard. He was playing football with a friend in Sheepy Road. They had to go to the Magistrate's Court. They were only schoolboys at the time, it was in 1923.

Maureen Barnes

Raising money for the football club

When my grandad was the trainer for Atherstone Town football club they won every cup and shield in everything they entered. When they had a football match, they would change at the Angel pub, then run down Sheepy Road to play football. After the game they would go back to the Angel to have a bath and change their clothes. My mother, Edie Hall, would have to collect their kit and take it to her mother, May Hall, so that she could wash it, iron it and have it ready for the following Saturday. Grandad was one of the first people to start raising money for the football club, which is where Bodacea's is now. I remember when it first started up. They had lots of odd chairs and a few odd tables and a piano.

Jean Neville

The Woodman

My dad, Fred Beale, and mother, Emma Beale, kept the Woodman Pub. It was on the corner of Station Street, opposite where the Co-op superstore is now. My sister Lola was born at the pub, I was born in a little house in Station Street, it isn't there anymore. Years ago there were houses, cottages, factories, businesses and the odd little sweet shop along Station Street and South Street. For years these streets were just as busy as Long Street. Dad run the pub and my mum went to work in the Finishing Shop at the hat factory to earn extra money. The pub only sold beer, no spirits, so there wasn't a lot of money to be made. I used to take my mother a jug of hot tea every day at

The Woodman pub, 1940s. Back row: -?- , J. Ford, -?- , B. Colclough, F. Beale, D. Cook. Front row: ? Barnes, -?- , B. Thumbwood, Alec Barnes, J. Thumwood, J. Pratt. Lola Beale is the little girl sitting at the front holding the cup.

lunchtime. My dad cooked the dinner and at five o'clock when my mother came home from work, we all sat down together. There was a great roaring fire in the pub during the winter, with great big pieces of coal glowing. I used to get the ashes up before I went to work. They were scrub-top tables and benches in the pub. Me, our Lola and my brother Eric used to help out with all the jobs, which had to be done. When my dad cleaned out the beer pipes with soda, we had to fetch and carry at least twenty buckets full of clean water to flush the pipes through. Up and down the cellar steps we had to go as there was no running water, just a tap in the yard. The deliverymen used to bring the barrels of beer on a horse and cart from Burton Ales. One of the men rolled the barrels down the cellar steps while the other man caught them and stacked them onto the cold thrawls. Now and again for some reason there would be a shortage of beer.

I remember my dad saying, 'Come on, we will go for a ride out in the car and go and have a drink in one of the country pubs. There will be enough beer to open up about 9.30 p.m. for the last hour.' When we came back in the car, the town looked dead. There was not a soul in sight, but as soon as the door was opened the people poured in, it felt like we had been invaded. You wondered where they all came from! The highlight of the year for us was the Bosworth Show, because any other special event or holiday meant more work for us. My dad closed the pub for half a day; it was the one time the whole family enjoyed a day out together.

Jean Beale

The Victor Silvester dances

Johnny Bickley used to take his gramophone and records to the Town Hall and teach us how to dance. We learned how to do the Victor Silvester dances – the Waltz and the Quick Step. Every so often there were proper dances at the Town Hall, where we could get all dressed up.

Rita Deeming

Atherstone Boys' Club FC

When I was at the Boys' Club we had a really good football team. Most of us played for Denham & Hargraves hat factory in the Trent Valley League.

Ron Lees

Harry Barnes trained the boxers

They used to spar at the Blue Bell pub, there was a room upstairs, a big concert room. Harry Barnes trained the boxers. There were a lot of boxers who came to Atherstone in the '30s, some very well-known boxers such as Randolph Turpin, all the big names that you would see in the newspapers. I just can't think of their names now, I was only a kid.

Derek Smith

Dozens of boxers

Just before the war you would find dozens of boxers in every city and town, only too willing to have a scrap, even if the reward was only the price of a hot meal and a pint. They were unemployed and a hungry man is always difficult to beat. In every boxing hall you would

Atherstone Boys' FC 1943/4. Back row: A. Croxall, H. Stubbs, T. Green, L. Barlow, F. Clamp, F. Barsby. Front row: C. Chapman, R. Lees, E. Round, B. Billingham, S. Bickley, D. Webster.

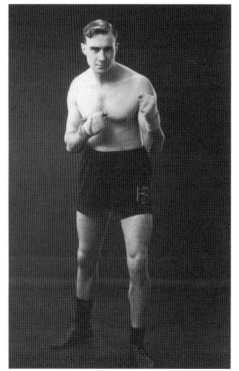

Above: Len Harvey, the British Cruiserweight Champion, and Jack Peterson, British Heavyweight Champion, 1930s.

Left: Harry Barnes in the 1930s.

The Town Hall in Market Street being demolished, August 1963.

find them queuing up, hoping someone on the bill hadn't turned up. Twenty fights under your belt meant you were a novice, you had to have one hundred fights notched up with most of them wins before being considered a 'top notcher'. Before the war, in 1939, there were 5,000 licensed boxers.

Harry Barnes

The circus came by train

My mum and dad had a shop at No. 10 Long Street. They sold lots of different things, it was a general store. When it was the Queen's Coronation, in 1953, we stood outside and watched the circus trainer and elephants walk up the middle of Long Street. They arrived by train at Atherstone train station. The train station was just over the road from the shop.

Jane Wykes

St Clements

Vero and Everritt's used to give their workers an orange and a lemon on St Clements Day, who was the patron saint of hatters. When it was Shrove Tuesday we were allowed to go out at 2.45 p.m. for the Ball Game. But we had to be back at 3.55 p.m. because the factory would all be locked up until five o'clock.

Jean Neville

A Tony Curtis haircut

If you wanted to be in fashion with a Tony Curtis haircut in the '60s, then Stephan's was the place to go, it cost 2s 6d. There used to be lots of cafés in Atherstone. There was the Clover café, Mann's café, the Calypso café and a couple more in the Market Place. We used to put two bob in the jukebox and get about six records played for that. We used to hang around in a gang and meet up in the cafés. Pickering's had a record shop in Long Street, we used to think it was great. We would go to the back of the shop and look through all the records. There was loads of pubs in the town and places to go for a dance. The Town Hall was a good place, the floorboards used to bounce though, its a wonder it didn't collapse. The Memorial Hall was good when it opened, a band called The Trend Men used to be on most Saturday nights. There's no doubt about it, Atherstone was always lively and people came from all over the place for a good night out. Can you remember the Bathing Bridge? We used to go swimming in the canal near the Bathing Bridge years ago. There used to be lots of people there on a Sunday afternoon and up the reser. The reser is filled in now, but it was nice up there, you could walk around the grass banks and find a good spot to sunbathe. Some of the lads used to swim to the island and back, it was a good way out and very dangerous really.

Horace Doherty

Coronation party

We all took something for the party; it was outside Cockey's café by the Avins yard and the Woodman pub. I can remember someone had made a trifle and we hadn't seen one for years, let alone eat one! The rationing was on until about 1956.

Jean Beale

JUNE 2nd, 1953   PRICE 1/-

SOUVENIR PROGRAMME

Celebrations
to be held in
ATHERSTONE
Warwickshire
on the occasion of the
Coronation of Her Majesty
Queen Elizabeth II

GOD SAVE THE QUEEN

Above: Atherstone Coronation Events Programme, 1953.

Left: A street party outside Cockey's café in 1953, near the Woodman pub in Station Street. Jean Beale is on the far right.

Employees of Vero's Knitwear held their Christmas Party in Lulu's Bar, the Old Red Lion Hotel, 1960. Jean Mills, Bet Russell, Iris Morris, Linda Deeming and Ivor Dawe are a few of the people in this happy crowd.

Christmas at Lulu's

I worked at Vero's Knitwear for years. The Knitwear was part of the original buildings of the hat factory, in Tenter Street. Every year we went to Lulu's Bar at the Red Lion for our Christmas parties. We used to have a great time.

Jean Mills

Have a Go at the Memorial Hall

The broadcast of Wilfred Pickles' *Have a Go* with 'Mabel at the Table' was conducted by the BBC when the Memorial Hall first opened in the 1960s. Wilfred Pickles autographed my ticket on the night.

Joyce Peart.

We could have danced all night

When the Memorial Hall opened they had dances on. We used to sit in the Calypso Bar over the road and wait for our friends to turn up. Then we would all go over to the dance together. I saw Screaming Lord Such, The Ronettes and the fifth Beatle – Pete Best.

Jean Neville

The Mods and Rockers Ball

The Mods used to hang around in the Calypso café opposite the Memorial Hall. We wore parkas and rode scooters. The Rockers wore black leather jackets and rode motorbikes. At the Memorial Hall we had what was called The Mods and Rockers Ball. It was disastrous, as the two were rivals, we clashed and didn't mix well at all. In later years the Mods and Rockers started to get on better. It was when Rocky King started to go around with the Atherstone Rockers, he was the leader. There was the occasional banter but nothing serious.

Trevor Chapman

Everlasting love

It was the '70s and John Smalley, who worked at the pit at the time, was selling tickets to see The Love Affair who were coming to Atherstone. John and some others from the pit had organised the venue at the Memorial Hall. It was a sell-out, we'd had some good bands play at the Memorial Hall, but none so famous. It was really exciting for us all. When The Love Affair had their interval, me and Donna Taylor ran over to the Calypso café where they were sitting and asked for their autographs. We were really nervous about asking them for their autographs. That night was a night we will never forget.

At about that time in the '70s, we used to go to Twycross Country Club, it used to be a great night out. Everyone met there once the pubs had shut in the town. There used to be a live band on until the early hours of the morning. A gang of us all went, we usually arranged our Friday nights out at work, when we worked at Denham Knitwear. Dot Gray organised the London trips and always sorted us out for the carnival. She would buy the material and cut out our costumes and we would machine them up on our sewing machines at work. We played the bazooka and marched one year. We did 'Up Pompeii' another year, Barbara Roberts from Sheepy Magna sorted us all out that year. She bought yards and yards of white silk material for our dresses and togas. It was a lovely float, we won second prize. I got more than I bargained for though! The Atherstone Rugby Club lads picked me up and threw me in a tank of horrible beer and water that was on their float. I'd spent ages getting ready with the other girls, I suppose it was all part of the fun.

Christine Freeman

The Statutes fair in the '60s

It was wonderful – apart from Atherstone Carnival it was the highlight of the year. Each September it came on the Back Way (Station Street). There were loads of side stalls where we tried to win prizes. But the favourites were the rides – the Waltzers, Ferris wheel and the Bumper Cars. When our money ran out, we'd all sit around the edge on the wooden railings watching everyone else and singing along to the latest chart songs that were played. All those songs of the '60s by The Beatles, The Stones, Billy J. Kramer, The Monkees and lots more. The men used to come and walk around from the pubs, so it was good if your dad was there, trying to win a coconut off the coconut shies. If you spotted your older brothers like I did, our John and Malcolm, they would pay for a ride or two. Friday was the best night to go because you got your pocket money and paper round money. It was payday for everyone. One year there was a new ride at the fair called The Twist, we thought it was great, 'Let's Twist Again' by Chubby Checker topped the charts. It didn't matter what new rides came with the fair, the Bumper Cars were always the best. The traditional Statutes stopped coming to the Back Way. They had to go on other car parks in the town and the playing fields. It was never the same, it lost that old excitement and charisma that the Statutes had had for years.

Christine Freeman

The Saturday matinee

Do you remember the old Picture House? It was next to Jenkins' bakery. We used to go to the bakery and buy a milk loaf and sit and eat it while we were watching the films. The manager at the time would announce who the winner was of the door ticket, he'd stand at the front. All the kids used to bombard him and throw their bits of leftover milk loaf at him. I know it's not nice, but you have to laugh.

Trevor Chapman

Mohican haircut

I can remember going to the Regal to watch Billy Two Rivers. There was me, Peter Groucott and Routlidge, now what's his first name? Do you know I just can't think what his first name was. Anyway, the barber was next door to the Regal – Bert Ford's place. We all went and had a Mohican haircut before we went inside to watch the wrestling. I thought it looked great, but when I got home the old lady went mad and told me 'You'd better go and get the lot off now'.

Horace Doherty

Carnival Queen

Mrs Trowman lived in Owen Street and was a seamstress. In 1947 Mrs Trowman made all

of the dresses for the Carnival Queen and the maids. She used floral plastic sheeting, which was really for making tablecloths with. Atherstone Carnival was one of the main events of the year. Everyone took part in decorating the shops, pubs and yards. We used everything and anything from flags to flowers. After the carnival procession was over a 'Fun Day' was held in a field by the Kings Head pub. There were games, rides, stalls and marching bands. It was great fun, the shops stayed open until ten o'clock at night.

Irene Northall

Third prize

We found an old carriage in a workshop in Coleshill Road. It was filthy but we all set

Arthur Lock, publican at the New Swan Inn, at the Atherstone Carnival, *c.* 1925.

Hilda Whelan, the 1947 Atherstone Carnival Queen, with Irene Northall (right) Mrs Trowman and Marge Deeming (back).

The 'Road Works Gang'; Nancy Clamp, Maisey Harrison, Sylvia Johnson, Gwen Johnson and Angela Johnson in the train station car park, 1962.

about cleaning it. The women made covers for the seats with old curtains. We won third prize at Atherstone and spent the £3 prize money in the pub afterwards. The carriage was bought by an interested party after the carnival, who restored it to its original condition.

Denis Fletcher

Atherstone Carnival

Atherstone Carnival was lovely, there were always lots of carnival floats every year. All the factories entered the carnival. 3M and BHS always put on a good float. Vonnie Wall always got the children together in York Avenue and did a wonderful dray. Then there were all the children who walked in the carnival in fancy dress. People did put a lot of effort into it – you could tell it must have taken them weeks to make all the costumes and decorations. My family came from Birmingham every year to watch the carnival, they had never seen anything like it. We used to sit on the grass opposite the cemetery, in Sheepy Road. The carnival just seemed to go on and on, float after float. It was good down the field afterwards in

'Horses for hire and funerals arranged'. Harold 'Bronc' Taft is the driver, with Ray Ward, Pam Allsopp, Denis Fletcher and Walter Grubb, in the 1960s.

The 1970s Ridge Lane Ladies' Club posing as the White Hart beauty queens over the decades of time, up to the year 2028.

Royal Meadow Drive. There were dancers, motorbike stunt riders, gymnastics and lots of other entertainment going on. The Scout Band made you feel ever so proud. Do you remember when it was the Queen's Silver Jubilee in 1977? Dave Lee Travis came, the Radio One DJ. It was a brilliant carnival that was and we all had street parties. The parties were all over the estate. It's such a shame we don't have the carnivals anymore.

Rita Bernard

Contributors of Photographs

I would like to thank most sincerely the following people for the loan of their personal photographs:

Roy Allitt
Sidney Barnes
Maureen Barnes
Gerry Barnes
Edward Arthur Byard
Amirian Byard
Geoff Butler
Jean Beale
Derek Booton
Janice Breedan
Bill Cooper
Bracebridge Court
Charles and Beryl Cooke
Trevor and Margaret Chapman
Eileen Colclough
Wilf Deeming
Horace Doherty
Janet Dingley
Maurice Douglas
Milly Evans
Gerald Eaton
Bill Ford
Beryl Freeman
Pat Fryer
Denis Fletcher

Gordon Gudger
Ernest Good
Gwen Heath
Ella Harrison
Eveline Johnson
Gwen Johnson
Iris Jones
Tom King
Margaret Killian
Nancy, Ron and Sylvia Lees
Ron Lees
Stuart Morcom
Jean Mills
Margaret Neale
Irene Northall
Joyce Peart
Charlie Ross
Dorothy Rushton
Joyce Reading
Celestine and Derek Smith
John Spragg
Paul Smith
Mavis Turner
Valda Wood
Margaret Wykes

Other local titles published by Tempus

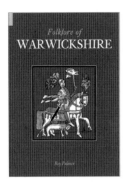

Folklore of Warwickshire
ROY PALMER

Warwickshire is a county steeped in tradition, folklore and mythology. This volume is a fascinating study of saints and sinners, sports and pastimes, fairs and wakes, folk song and balladry, the passage rites of marriage, birth and death, omens and superstitions, all coloured by the horror of witchcraft and the supernatural.

0 7524 3359 8

Nuneaton Volume II
PETER LEE

This absorbing collection provides a nostalgic glimpse into the history of Nuneaton during the last century. Compiled with over 160 photographs and postcards, this selection highlights some of the changes and events that have taken place in the town. From glimpses of working life, including cotton, textiles and engineering industries, through to the modernisation of the town during the 1950s and '60s, each image recalls the social history of Nuneaton.

0 7524 3242 7

The City of Coventry
GRAHAM KEMPSTER

Illustrated with 170 old photographs this volume highlights some of the important events that have occurred in the city of Coventry during the last century, including blitz bombing during the Second World War and the arrival of the railway at the end of the nineteenth century. Aspects of everyday life are also featured, from schools and churches, streets and shops, to sporting events and leisure pursuits.

0 7524 3357 1

Catholics in Birmingham
CHRISTINE WARD-PENNY

With 200 photographs, many from the archives of Birmingham Central Library, this book records the remarkable growth of the Catholic community in Birmingham during the nineteenth century and captures the flavour of what Roman Catholics have brought to the city. Today there are ten of thousands of Catholics in the Birmingam and this book is dedicated to their history and traditions.

0 7524 3362 8

If you are interested in purchasing other books published by Tempus, or in case you have difficulty finding any Tempus books in your local bookshop, you can also place orders directly through our website

www.tempus-publishing.com